German Vocabulary by Topic

Philip and Ursula Horsfall

MARY GLASGOW PUBLICATIONS

We are grateful to the following for allowing us to reproduce published material:

ADAC Motorwelt (p. 50); Bremer Tageszeitungen AG (pp. 36, 39); Dr. Burg (p. 24); Düsseldorfer Illustrierte (pp. 64, 80); Firma Kika St. Poelten (p. 41); Frankfurter Allgemeine (pp. 9, 79); Frau mit Herz (p. 12); Fremdenverkehrszentrale Hamburg e.V. (pp. 26, 76); Die Glocke (p. 39); Herbert und Elfi Rist (p. 54); Horst Böhler Verlagsservice (p. 37); Hotel Alpenrose, Oetz (p. 54); Kasseler Sonntagsblatt (p. 18); Kettelhack Rikcr Pharma GmbH (p. 72); Köln-Düsseldorfer Deutsche Rheinschiffahrt AG (p. 18); Möbel Märki (p. 24); Oberösterreichische Nachrichten (pp. 18, 36, 69); Saarbrücker Zeitung (pp. 56, 57, 58); Schweizer Familie (p. 26); Schweizer Woche (p. 9); Stern (p. 42); Süddeutsche Zeitung (p. 22); Südwest Presse Ulm (pp. 22, 41, 71, 74); TV Hören und Sehen (p. 34); Unser Schaffen (p. 9); Vademecum (p. 72); Verkehrsamt Rüdesheim am Rhein (pp. 56, 74); Verlag Deutsches Jugendherbergswerk (p. 57); Wildpark Nindorf (p. 26).

Every effort has been made to trace the copyright holders but the publishers will be pleased to make the necessary arrangements at the first opportunity if there are any omissions.

Design: Penny Mills
Cover design: Ingrid Emsden

Photographs: Dietmar Binkert, David Simson, Presse-Bild-Poss, Ulrich P. Wienke
and Mary Glasgow Publications

First published 1989
Reprinted 1990, 1991 (twice), 1992, 1993, 1994

Mary Glasgow Publications
An imprint of Stanley Thornes (Publishers) Ltd
Ellenborough House
Wellington Street
CHELTENHAM GL50 1YD

Photoset in Linotron Plantin with Helvetica by Northern Phototypesetting Co, Bolton

Printed by Martin's The Printers Ltd., Berwick upon Tweed

Contents

Introduction

This short vocabulary book has one simple aim – to give you a topic-by-topic checklist of the words you will need to know for your examination.

The vocabulary is divided into two sections:

Basic vocabulary
(listed as English to German)

These are key words, words you need to have actively at your command. You should be able to use them naturally when you speak German.

Higher vocabulary
(listed as English to German)

These are words that candidates tackling the higher parts of the exam should know actively in addition to all the basic vocabulary.

You will see whether a word is masculine, feminine or neuter from the use of *der*, *die* and *das*. The plural of all nouns which have a plural form is given in brackets, for example: *die Frau(en)*, *der Mann(¨er)*, *das Kind(er)*. Where it is not clear from the English whether a noun has a plural form or not, this is also indicated in brackets (*no pl*), e.g. *das Ausland (no pl)*. Nouns which are always plural are marked (*pl*), e.g. *die Möbel (pl)*, and (-) means the noun stays the same in the plural, e.g. *das Poster(-)*.
Verbs which are separable are marked (*sep*), for example: *zuhören (sep) – ich höre*

zu. In some cases, the preposition which follows a verb is given, for example: *telefonieren mit (+ dat)*.
Colloquial expressions are marked *coll:*, for example: *fotografieren, coll: knipsen*.

The words are not listed in long alphabetical chunks. They are grouped in short blocks of words that go together in some way. This is designed to make your revision more logical and to make it easier for your teacher to set learning or revision homeworks.

Phrases
Near the end of each topic you will find examples of phrases – **Basic Phrases** and **Higher Phrases** – that you might hear or need in the oral exam. Practise reading them aloud, then cover the German and say the phrase using the English translation as a prompt.

Signs and notices
For most topics, there is a final section on signs and notices. These are usually, though not always, based on words from the list. Test yourself by trying to work out what they mean.

This book is a revision guide, a checklist, a consolidation and reference book. It is not a teaching book, nor can it be totally comprehensive. The examining boards say that five per cent of the words used in the exams may come from outside lists such as these. Remember, too, that learning vocabulary is only one part of preparing for an exam. We can't promise you instant success, but if you are confident you can use or recognise all the words in this book in appropriate situations, you are certainly one step closer to a good exam result.

Good luck!

1 Talking about yourself and others

Personal details

BASIC VOCABULARY

to be called	**heißen**
to name	**nennen**
first name	**der Vorname**(n)
surname	**der Nachname**(n)
to sign	**unterschreiben**
signature	**die Unterschrift**(en)
old	**alt**
young	**jung**
birthday	**der Geburtstag**(e)
date of birth	**das Geburtsdatum** (daten)
month	**der Monat**(e)
year	**das Jahr**(e)
to live	**wohnen**
house	**das Haus**(¨er)
flat	**die Wohnung**(en)
address	**die Adresse**(n), **die Anschrift**(en)
road, street	**die Straße**(n)
avenue	**die Allee**(n)
(house) number	**die (Haus)nummer**(n)

town, city	**die Stadt**(¨e)
village	**das Dorf**(¨er)
country	**das Land**(¨er) (also region in Germany)

HIGHER VOCABULARY

maiden name	**der Mädchenname**(n)
to spell	**buchstabieren**
born, née	**geboren**(e)
place of birth	**der Geburtsort**(e)
age	**das Alter** (no pl)
adult	**der Erwachsene**(n)
young person	**der Jungendliche**(n)
gender, sex	**das Geschlecht**(er)
male	**männlich**
female	**weiblich**
postcode	**die Postleitzahl**(en)
home town	**die Heimatstadt** (¨e)
home town/country	**die Heimat** (no pl)

BASIC PHRASES

I'm called Jo and I'm 15.	**Ich heiße Jo und ich bin 15 Jahre alt.**
I was born in Liverpool in 1973.	**Ich bin 1973 in Liverpool geboren.**
My birthday is on June 10th.	**Mein Geburtstag ist am zehnten Juni.**
	Ich habe am zehnten Juni Geburtstag.
I live near York.	**Ich wohne in der Nähe von York.**

7

HIGHER PHRASES

Could you spell your name, please?	**Können Sie bitte Ihren Namen buchstabieren?**
My name is written with two ls.	**Mein Name schreibt sich mit zwei L.**
I don't know the postcode.	**Ich weiß die Postleitzahl nicht.**
My home town is Norwich.	**Meine Heimatstadt ist Norwich.**

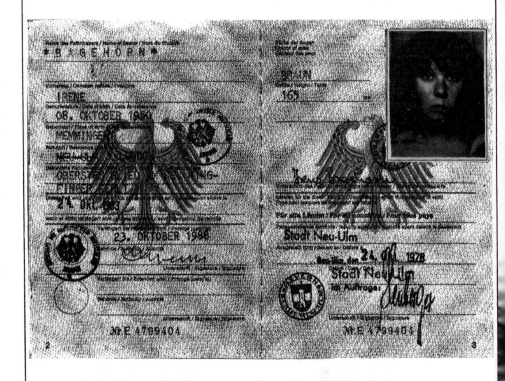

Nationality and religion

BASIC VOCABULARY

Germany	**Deutschland**	an Austrian	**ein Österreicher(-)**
a German	**ein Deutscher** (Deutschen)	Austrian	**österreichisch**
German	**deutsch**	Switzerland	**die Schweiz**
England	**England**	a Swiss	**ein Schweizer(-)**
an Englishman	**ein Engländer(-)**	Swiss	**schweizerisch**
English	**englisch**	Belgium	**Belgien**
Austria	**Österreich**	a Belgian	**ein Belgier(-)**

(BASIC VOCABULARY)		HIGHER VOCABULARY	
Belgian	**belgisch**	religion	**die Religion**(en)
France	**Frankreich**	Protestant	**protestantisch,**
a Frenchman	**ein Franzose**(n)		**evangelisch**
French	**französisch**	Catholic	**katholisch**
Holland	**Holland**	Moslem	**mohammedanisch**
a Dutchman	**ein Holländer**(-)	service	**der Gottesdienst**(e)
Dutch	**holländisch**		
Italy	**Italien**	abroad	**das Ausland** (*no pl*)
an Italian	**ein Italiener**(-)	foreigner	**der Ausländer**(-),
Italian	**italienisch**		**die Ausländerin**(nen)
Spain	**Spanien**	nationality	**die Staatsange-**
a Spaniard	**ein Spanier**(-)		**hörigkeit**(en)
Spanish	**spanisch**	Great Britain	**Großbritannien**
America	**Amerika**	to come from	**stammen aus** (+ *dat*)
an American	**ein Amerikaner**		
American	**amerikanisch**		

*NB The feminine form of the above nouns
always adds -in(nen), eg* **eine Holländerin,**
except: **eine Deutsche(n), eine Französin**

Where do these newspapers/magazines come from?

*Jänner is Austrian for **Januar**

9

BASIC PHRASES

I come from England.	**Ich komme aus England.**
I'm English.	**Ich bin Engländer(in).**
Where do you come from?	**Wo kommst du her?**
	Woher kommst du?
Are you German?	**Sind Sie Deutsche(r)?**
Do you speak English?	**Sprechen Sie Englisch?**

HIGHER PHRASES

I come from the south of England.	**Ich stamme aus Südengland.**
I have never been abroad.	**Ich bin noch nie im Ausland gewesen.**
I'm Protestant.	**Ich bin evangelisch.**

Appearance

BASIC VOCABULARY

big (tall)	**groß**		grey	**grau**
medium sized	**mittelgroß**		green	**grün**
small	**klein**		black	**schwarz**
fat	**dick**		white	**weiß**
thin	**dünn**			
ugly	**häßlich**		to look, appear	**aussehen** (*sep*)
pretty	**hübsch**		to recognise	**erkennen**
beautiful	**schön**		beard	**der Bart(¨e)**
strong	**stark**		glasses, spectacles	**die Brille(n)**
weak	**schwach**		hair	**das Haar(e)**
long	**lang**		eye	**das Auge(n)**
short	**kurz**			
round	**rund**			
dark	**dunkel**		**HIGHER VOCABULARY**	
light	**hell**		(very) thin	**mager**
blue	**blau**		pale	**blaß**
blond	**blond**		moustache	**der Schnurrbart(¨e)**
brown	**braun**		similar	**ähnlich**

BASIC PHRASES

She is very pretty.	**Sie ist sehr hübsch.**
She wears glasses.	**Sie trägt eine Brille.**
I've got dark brown hair.	**Ich habe dunkelbraunes Haar.**
What sort of car do you have?	**Was für ein Auto hast du?**
I'm fairly tall.	**Ich bin ziemlich groß.**

HIGHER PHRASES

He's got a thin moustache.	**Er hat einen dünnen Schnurrbart.**
She is very similar to me.	**Sie ist mir sehr ähnlich.**
What does your mother look like?	**Wie sieht deine Mutter aus?**
You look very pale.	**Du siehst sehr blaß aus.**

Character and feelings

BASIC VOCABULARY

good	**gut**
bad	**schlimm, schlecht**
nice	**nett**
friendly	**freundlich**
unfriendly	**unfreundlich**
funny	**komisch, lustig**
to smile	**lächeln**
to laugh	**lachen**
happy	**glücklich**
sad	**traurig**
quiet, calm	**ruhig**
angry	**böse**
lazy	**faul**
hardworking	**fleißig**
clever	**intelligent**
stupid	**dumm**
fear	**die Angst(¨e)**
to think	**denken**
to hope	**hoffen**
to want, wish	**wollen**
to surprise	**überraschen**
surprise	**die Überraschung (en)**
rich	**reich**
poor	**arm**

HIGHER VOCABULARY

honest	**ehrlich**
polite	**höflich**
likeable	**sympathisch**
sensible	**vernünftig**
keen	**begeistert**
lively	**lebhaft**
shy	**schüchtern**
naughty	**ungezogen**
silly	*coll:* **blöd, doof**
in a good/bad mood	**gut/schlecht gelaunt**
nervous	**nervös**
curious (nosy)	**neugierig**
cheeky	**frech**
furious	**wütend**
to get on with someone	**sich mit jemandem vertragen**
to dislike someone	**jemanden nicht leiden können**
to disappoint	**enttäuschen**
disappointment	**die Enttäuschung(en)**
to be right	**recht haben**
to be wrong	**unrecht haben**
to guess	**(er)raten**

BASIC PHRASES

I'm afraid.	**Ich habe Angst.**
I want to be rich.	**Ich will reich sein.**
He's not as nice as his brother.	**Er ist nicht so nett wie sein Bruder.**
I think I'm quite lazy.	**Ich glaube, ich bin ziemlich faul.**

HIGHER PHRASES

I get on well with my parents.	**Ich vertrage mich gut mit meinen Eltern.**
I think I'm always right.	**Ich glaube, daß ich immer recht habe.**
Yesterday I was in a bad mood.	**Gestern war ich schlecht gelaunt.**
I can't stand him.	**Ich kann ihn nicht leiden.**
She is a shy but likeable girl.	**Sie ist ein schüchternes aber sympathisches Mädchen.**

Star signs!

Des sagen die Sterne für die Woche vom 17. 9. bis 23. 9. voraus

Ihr Glücks-/Horoskop

Zwillinge

21. Mai—21. Juni
Sie haben jetzt viel Bewegungsfreiheit, und es gibt Aufgaben, die Ihnen Freude machen. Jupiter und Mars bringen den Geborenen der 1. Dekade positive Veränderungen. Sie erreichen die gewünschte Aufmerksamkeit. Auch die Junidaten dürfen alle Bedenken über Bord werfen.

Widder

21. März—20. April
Eine weitere Woche, die fast ganz nach Ihren Vorstellungen verläuft. Im Beruf bietet sich Gelegenheit, Ihr Können herauszustreichen. Privat haben Sie Zeit, an die Verwirklichung ganz persönlicher Wünsche zu gehen. Auch wenn Ihnen eine Einladung ungelegen kommt, sollten Sie hingehen.

Stier

21. April—20. Mai
Vergnügen und Ablenkungen können Sie in diesen Tagen mit Ihren Pflichten in Konflikt bringen. Dabei ist Gründlichkeit jetzt besonders wichtig, sonst sind Sie im Nachteil. Halten Sie sich mit Ausgaben zurück, und seien Sie vorsichtig, wenn Ihnen jemand ein Bombengeschäft verspricht.

Waage

24. Sept.—23. Okt.
Die Tage sind recht anregend und abwechslungsreich, und vor allem im Bereich von Freundschaft und Liebe erfahren Sie viel Angenehmes. Merkur und Venus fördern die Pflege geselliger Beziehungen, machen Sie aufnahmebereit für Vergnügen und Kunstgenuß.

Skorpion

24. Okt.—22. Nov.
Ihr Ehrgeiz in beruflichen Dingen sollte nicht Ihr ganzes Denken bestimmen. Es wäre jetzt besser, sich von manchen Dingen zu distanzieren, da es kaum etwas bringt, nur forsch oder gar gewaltsam die eigenen Pläne vorantreiben zu wollen. Mit der Liebe will es nicht so recht klappen.

Krebs

22. Juni—22. Juli
Im Berufsleben gibt es manche Hürde, Verpflichtungen nehmen überhand und werden als lästig empfunden. Eine unvorhergesehene Rechnung könnte Ihre Finanzen ganz schön durcheinander bringen. In der Liebe gibt es Unklarheiten. Ein Gespräch mit dem Partner verschafft Klarheit.

Löwe

23. Juli—23. August
Monoton wird die Woche keinesfalls. Sie haben viel Schwung und können Ihre berufliche Position festigen. Geistig anregende Aspekte, die vor allem auch die Anknüpfung und Pflege persönlicher Beziehungen begünstigen, halten an. Auch der Liebesstern steht günstig.

Daily routine

BASIC VOCABULARY

to wake up	aufwachen *(sep)*
to get up	aufstehen *(sep)*
to go to the toilet	auf die Toilette gehen
to have a wash	sich waschen
to get dressed	sich anziehen *(sep)*
to get undressed	sich ausziehen *(sep)*
to wear	tragen
to make the bed	das Bett machen
to have breakfast	frühstücken
to eat	essen
to drink	trinken
lunch	das Mittagessen(-)
dinner	das Abendessen(-)
supper	das Abendbrot(e)
to have lunch	zu Mittag essen
to have dinner	zu Abend essen
to cook	kochen
to lay the table	den Tisch decken
to clear the table	den Tisch abräumen *(sep)*
to prepare	vorbereiten *(sep)*
to help	helfen
to sit, be sitting	sitzen
to sit down	sich setzen
to have a seat	Platz nehmen
to stand	stehen
to sleep	schlafen
to watch TV	fernsehen *(sep)*

to have a shower	duschen
to open	öffnen, aufmachen *(sep)*
to close	schließen, zumachen *(sep)*
to bring	bringen
to take	nehmen
to clean	saubermachen *(sep)*, putzen
to wash up	abwaschen *(sep)*
to leave	verlassen

HIGHER VOCABULARY

awake	wach
to wake up	aufwachen *(sep)*
to wake someone up	jemanden aufwecken *(sep)*
to fall asleep	einschlafen *(sep)*
to chat	plaudern, sich unterhalten
to talk	reden
to get changed	sich umziehen *(sep)*
to lie down	sich hinlegen *(sep)*
to comb one's hair	sich kämmen
to brush one's hair	seine Haare bürsten, sich das Haar bürsten
brush	die Bürste(n)
comb	der Kamm("e)
hairdryer	der Fön(e)

BASIC PHRASES

I get up at 7 o'clock.	Ich stehe um sieben Uhr auf.
In the morning I always eat toast.	Morgens esse ich immer Toast.
I watch TV or I help in the kitchen.	Ich sehe fern oder helfe in der Küche.
When do you go to bed?	Wann gehst du ins Bett?
We have dinner together.	Wir essen zusammen zu Abend.

HIGHER PHRASES

Can I help with the washing up?	**Kann ich beim Abwaschen helfen?**
The first thing I do is get changed.	**Als erstes ziehe ich mich um.**
I look after the dog.	**Ich kümmere mich um den Hund.**
Usually I fall asleep at about 11.	**Gewöhnlich schlafe ich gegen 11 Uhr ein.**
I clean my own room.	**Ich mache mein Zimmer selbst sauber.**

Family

BASIC VOCABULARY

Mr	**Herr**
Mrs	**Frau**
Miss	**Fräulein**
family	**die Familie(n)**
friend	**der Freund(e),**
	die Freundin(nen)
to marry	**heiraten**
married	**verheiratet**
divorced	**geschieden**
engaged	**verlobt**
fiancé(e)	**der/die Verlobte(n)**

mother	**die Mutter(¨)**
mum	**Mutti**
father	**der Vater(¨)**
dad	**Vati**
parents	**die Eltern**
husband	**der (Ehe)mann(¨er)**
wife	**die (Ehe)frau(en)**
child	**das Kind(er)**
baby	**das Baby(s)**
son	**der Sohn(¨e)**
daughter	**die Tochter(¨)**

grandparents	**die Großeltern**
grandfather	**der Großvater(¨)**
grandad	**der Opa(s)**
grandmother	**die Großmutter(¨)**
grandma	**die Oma(s), die Omi(s)**
grandson	**der Enkel(-)**

granddaughter	**die Enkelin(nen)**

brother	**der Bruder(¨)**
sister	**die Schwester(n)**
brothers and/or sisters	**die Geschwister**
boy	**der Junge(n)**
girl	**das Mädchen(-)**
uncle	**der Onkel(-)**
aunt	**die Tante(n)**

HIGHER VOCABULARY

relative	**der Verwandte(n)**
cousin (male)	**der Cousin(s),**
	der Vetter(n)
cousin (female)	**die Cousine(n),**
	die Kusine(n)
nephew	**der Neffe(n)**
niece	**die Nichte(n)**
single, unmarried	**ledig**
married couple	**das Ehepaar(e)**
widow	**die Witwe(n)**
widower	**der Witwer(-)**

brother-in-law	**der Schwager(¨)**
sister-in-law	**die Schwägerin(nen)**
father-in-law	**der Schwiegervater(¨)**
mother-in-law	**die Schwiegermutter(¨)**

BASIC PHRASES

I've got one brother and two sisters.	**Ich habe einen Bruder und zwei Schwestern.**
Have you got any brothers or sisters?	**Hast du Geschwister?**
I don't know his sister.	**Ich kenne seine Schwester nicht.**
I live with my mother.	**Ich wohne bei meiner Mutter.**
This is my father.	**Das ist mein Vater.**

HIGHER PHRASES

I'm an only child.	**Ich bin ein Einzelkind.**
All my relatives live near here.	**Alle meine Verwandten wohnen in der Nähe.**
My elder sister is not married.	**Meine ältere Schwester ist ledig.**
I'm the youngest in the family.	**Ich bin der/die Jüngste in der Familie.**

Telephone

BASIC VOCABULARY

telephone	**das Telefon(e),** **der Fernsprecher(-)** *(public telephones only)*
to ring up	**telefonieren mit** (+ *dat*), **anrufen** (+ *acc*) (*sep*)
telephone booth	**die Telefonzelle(n)**
directory	**das Telefonbuch("er)**
telephone number	**die Telefon-nummer(n)**
dialling code	**die Vorwahl(en),** **die Vorwahlnummer(n)**
speaking, on the line	**am Apparat**
to talk to	**sprechen mit** (+ *dat*)
receiver	**der Hörer(-)**
to dial	**wählen**

to dial a wrong number	**falsch wählen,** **sich verwählen**
engaged	**besetzt**

HIGHER VOCABULARY

to get a wrong number	**falsch verbunden sein**
a connection	**die Verbindung(en)**
conversation	**das Gespräch(e)**
local call	**das Ortsgespräch(e)**
long distance call	**das Ferngespräch(e)**
reversed charge call	**das R-Gespräch(e)**
by telephone	**telefonisch**

BASIC PHRASES

My telephone number is 2405.	**Meine Telefonnumer ist vierundzwanzig null fünf.**
What is the code for Mainz?	**Was ist die Vorwahl von Mainz?**
Can I ring my parents?	**Kann ich meine Eltern anrufen?**
Who's speaking?	**Wer ist am Apparat?**

HIGHER PHRASES

Can I get you on the phone?	**Kann ich Sie telefonisch erreichen?**
You've got the wrong number.	**Sie sind falsch verbunden.**
Could I make a reversed charge call?	**Könnte ich ein R-Gespräch führen?**
Please hold the line!	**Bitte warten!**

What do these signs tell you?

2 Socialising

BASIC VOCABULARY

good morning	**guten Morgen**
hello	**guten Tag, grüß Gott**, *coll:* **Servus, Tag**
good evening	**guten Abend**
good night	**gute Nacht**
goodbye	**auf Wiedersehen, Tschüß** (*less formal*), **auf Wiederhören** (*telephone*)
welcome	**herzlich willkommen**
see you later	**bis später**
see you soon	**bis bald**
see you tomorrow	**bis morgen**
Happy Easter	**frohe Ostern**
Happy Christmas	**frohe Weihnachten**
Happy New Year	**ein glückliches neues Jahr**
Happy Birthday	**herzlichen Glückwunsch zum Geburtstag**
same to you	**gleichfalls**
have a good time	**viel Spaß!**
good luck	**viel Glück!**
enjoy your meal	**Mahlzeit! Guten Appetit!**
safe journey	**gute Reise, gute Fahrt**
have a safe journey home	**komm gut nach Hause**
get well soon	**gute Besserung**
all the best	**mach's gut, alles Gute**
sweet dreams	**träume süß, träum' schön**
goodness!	**Himmel! Ach du lieber Gott! Mein Gott! Mensch! Du meine Güte!**
yes indeed, willingly	**gerne**
I hope so	**hoffentlich**

unfortunately	**leider**
isn't it great?	**ist es nicht toll, prima, wunderbar?**
terrible	**furchtbar, schrecklich**
cheers!	**Prost!**
nonsense!	**Quatsch! Blödsinn!**
damn!	**verdammt!**
thanks, thank you	**vielen Dank**
you're welcome, not at all	**nichts zu danken, bitte**
no idea	**keine Ahnung**
look out!	**Vorsicht! Achtung!**
definitely	**bestimmt**
really?	**wirklich?**

HIGHER VOCABULARY

agreed	**abgemacht, einverstanden**
understood, got it	**kapiert, begriffen, verstanden**
not at all	**gar nicht**
bad luck	**Pech**
sorry	**Verzeihung**
pity	**schade**
cheers!	**zum Wohl!**
have fun	**viel Vergnügen**
congratulations	**ich gratuliere**
delighted (to meet you)	**es freut mich (Sie kennenzulernen)**
to refuse	**ablehnen** (*sep*)
to accept	**annehmen** (*sep*)
to ask	**bitten**
to recommend	**empfehlen**
to be all right, to 'work'	*coll:* **klappen**
to succeed	**gelingen**
to guess	**raten**

17

(HIGHER VOCABULARY)

to take one's leave	**sich verabschieden**	to use the 'du' form	**(sich) duzen**
to prefer	**vorziehen** *(sep)*	to use the 'Sie' form	**(sich) siezen**
to intend	**vorhaben** *(sep)*	I am in favour	**ich habe nichts dagegen, ich bin dafür**
to surprise	**überraschen**		
to meet	**(sich) treffen** *(mit + dat)*	with pleasure	**mit Vergnügen**
		satisfied	**zufrieden**

Personelles

Geburtstage

In **Linz** vollenden heute, Samstag, Gertraud Unger, Elisabethstraße 23, das 85.; Franziska Kiesenebner und Katharina Stierbacher, beide Glimpfingerstraße 10, das 90. Lebensjahr.

Goldene Hochzeit

In Linz feiern heute die Ehepaare Rosa und Josef Eder, Poschacherstraße 5, und Stefanie und Maximilian Heinisch, Blindwiesen 28, das Fest der goldenen Hochzeit.

Gestorben ist der surrealistische Künstler Salvador Dali (84).

In Liebe und Dankbarkeit nehmen wir Abschied von meinem lieben Gatten, Bruder, Schwager und Onkel, Herrn

JOSEF PHILIPP
Magistratsbeamter in Ruhe

welcher am Donnerstag, dem 2. Februar 1989, nach kurzer, schwerer Krankheit im 68. Lebensjahr von Gott abberufen wurde.

Herzlich willkommen

3 House and home

General description

to live	**wohnen**
to rent	**mieten**
to buy	**kaufen**
to sell	**verkaufen**
to change	**wechseln**
to build	**bauen**

house	**das Haus(¨er)**
semi-detached house	**das Doppelhaus(¨er)**
detached house	**das Einfamilienhaus(¨er)**
terraced house	**das Reihenhaus(¨er)**
block of flats	**der (Wohn)block(¨e)**
bungalow	**der Bungalow(s)**
building	**das Gebäude(-)**
farm	**der Bauernhof(¨e)**

front door	**die Haustür(en)**
key	**der Schlüssel(-)**
to ring	**läuten, klingeln**
to knock	**(an)klopfen** (*sep*)
window	**das Fenster(-)**
wall	**die Mauer(n)** (*outside*), **die Wand(¨e)** (*inside*)
storey	**die Etage(n)**, **der Stock (Stockwerke)**
floor	**der Boden (¨)**

old	**alt**
new	**neu**
modern	**modern**
large	**groß**
small	**klein**
comfortable	**bequem**
upstairs	**oben**
downstairs	**unten**
stairs	**die Treppe(n)**

garden	**der Garten (¨)**
gardening	**die Gartenarbeit (en)**
yard	**der Hof(¨e)**
flower	**die Blume(n)**
plant	**die Pflanze(n)**
vegetable(s)	**das Gemüse**
grass	**das Gras(¨er)**
tree	**der Baum(¨e)**
fruit tree	**der Obstbaum(¨e)**

owner-occupied flat	**die Eigentumswohnung(en)**
multi-storey building	**das Hochhaus(¨er)**
position	**die Lage(n)**
view	**die Aussicht, der Blick**
ground floor	**das Erdgeschoß(sse)**
upper floor	**das Obergeschoß(sse)**
comfortable, cosy	**gemütlich**
square yard (*approx*)	**der Quadratmeter(-)**

roof	**das Dach(¨er)**
ceiling	**die Decke(n)**
(central) heating	**die (Zentral) heizung(en)**
to heat	**heizen**
to move house	**umziehen** (*sep*)
to wallpaper	**tapezieren**
wallpaper	**die Tapete(n)**
to paint	**(an)streichen** (*sep*)

to water	**gießen**
to mow	**mähen**
lawn	**der Rasen(-)**
to grow	**wachsen**
garden tools	**die Gartengeräte**
terrace	**die Terrasse(n)**
gate	**das Tor(e)**

What do these signs mean?

BASIC PHRASES

I live in a semi.	**Ich wohne in einem Doppelhaus.**
I don't like gardening	**Gartenarbeit gefällt mir nicht.**
Our house has got two storeys.	**Unser Haus hat zwei Etagen**
Do you live in a house or a flat?	**Wohnst du in einem Haus oder in einer Wohnung?**
Our garden isn't very big.	**Unser Garten ist nicht sehr groß**

HIGHER PHRASES

We live in our own flat.	**Wir wohnen in einer Eigentumswohnung.**
Our garden is about 40 square yards.	**Unser Garten hat etwa 40 Quadratmeter.**
We want to move house.	**Wir wollen umziehen.**
Lots of vegetables grow in our garden.	**In unserem Garten wächst viel Gemüse.**
The bathroom is on the ground floor.	**Das Badezimmer ist im Erdgeschoß.**

Rooms and services

BASIC VOCABULARY

space	**der Platz**(no pl)
garage	**die Garage**(n)
cellar	**der Keller**(-)
hall	**der Flur**(e)
staircase	**das Treppenhaus**(¨er)
room	**der Raum**(¨e), **das Zimmer**(-)
bathroom	**das Badezimmer**(-)
dining room	**das Eßzimmer**(-)
living room	**das Wohnzimmer**(-)
bedroom	**das Schlafzimmer**(-)
toilet	**die Toilette**(n)
kitchen	**die Küche**(n)
electricity	**die Elektrizität**
gas	**das Gas**
oil	**das Öl**
water	**das Wasser**

tap	**der Hahn**(¨e)
button	**der Knopf**(¨e)
to switch on	**anmachen** (sep)
to switch off	**ausmachen** (sep)

HIGHER VOCABULARY

attic	**der Dachboden**(¨)
corridor	**der Gang**(¨e)
socket	**die Steckdose**(n)
plug	**der Stecker**(-)
electric current	**der Strom**
bulb	**die Glühbirne**(n)
candle	**die Kerze**(n)
coal	**die Kohle**(n)
switch	**der Schalter**(-)
to switch on	**einschalten** (sep)
to switch off	**ausschalten** (sep)

BASIC PHRASES

I have my own room.	**Ich habe mein eigenes Zimmer.**
We don't have a cellar.	**Wir haben keinen Keller**

(BASIC PHRASES)

There are three bedrooms.	**Es gibt drei Schlafzimmer.**
The bathroom is upstairs to the right.	**Das Badezimmer ist oben rechts.**
Where do I switch the light on?	**Wo mache ich das Licht an?**

HIGHER PHRASES

We'll tell you when the bathroom is free.	**Wir sagen dir, wenn das Badezimmer frei ist.**
The toilet is at the end of the corridor.	**Die Toilette ist am Ende des Ganges.**
There is a power cut.	**Der Strom ist ausgefallen.**

**What kind of accommodation is for
sale?**

Furniture and equipment

BASIC VOCABULARY

furniture	die Möbel (*pl*)
bed	das Bett(en)
bedding	das Bettzeug
alarm clock	der Wecker(-)
chair	der Stuhl(¨e)
chest of drawers	die Kommode(n)
wardrobe	der Kleiderschrank(¨e)
clothes brush	die Kleiderbürste(n)
lamp	die Lampe(n)
poster	das Poster(-)

cooker	der Herd(e)
refrigerator	der Kühlschrank(¨e)
washing machine	die Waschmaschine(n)
table	der Tisch(e)
appliance	der Apparat(e)
plate	der Teller(-)
cup	die Tasse(n)
glass	das Glas(¨er)
knife	das Messer(-)
fork	die Gabel(n)
spoon	der Löffel(-)
teapot	die Teekanne(n)
coffee pot	die Kaffeekanne(n)

bath	das Bad(¨er)
bath tub	die Badewanne(n)
shower	die Dusche(n)
light	das Licht(er)
shampoo	das Shampoo(s), das Haarwaschmittel(-)
toilet paper	das Toilettenpapier (*no pl*)
toothbrush	die Zahnbürste(n)
toothpaste	die Zahnpasta(pasten)
soap	die Seife(n)
towel	das Handtuch(¨er)

picture	das Bild(er)
settee, sofa	die Couch(s)
armchair	der Sessel(-)

television	der Fernsehapparat(e), der Fernseher(-)
video	das Videogerät(e)
stereo	die Stereoanlage(n)
clock	die Uhr(en)
standard lamp	die Stehlampe(n)

HIGHER VOCABULARY

blanket	die Decke(n)
sheet	das Bettlaken(-), das Bettuch(¨er)
sheets	die Bettwäsche
feather bed	das Federbett(en)
pillow	das Kopfkissen(-)
duvet	die Steppdecke(n)

curtain	der Vorhang(¨e)
net curtain	die Gardine(n)
blind	das Rollo(s)
carpet	der Teppich(e)
bedside table	der Nachttisch(e)
mirror	der Spiegel(-)
dressing table	die Frisierkommode(n)

(waste paper) bin	der (Abfall)eimer(-)
to throw away	wegwerfen (*sep*)
vacuum cleaner	der Staubsauger(-)
dishwasher	die (Geschirr)spülmaschine(n)
washing-up liquid	das Spülmittel(-)
bowl	die Schüssel(n)
dish	die Schale(n)
pot	der Topf(¨e)
crockery	das Geschirr
table cloth	die Tischdecke(n)
washing powder	das Waschpulver(-)
freezer	die Tiefkühltruhe(n)
oven	der Ofen(¨)

(HIGHER VOCABULARY)

tray	**das Tablett**(s)	washbasin	**das Waschbecken**(-)
ashtray	**der Aschenbecher**(-)	face cloth	**der Waschlappen**(-)
		shelf	**das Regal**(e)
shaver	**der Rasierapparat**(e)		

BASIC PHRASES

We've got a colour TV.	**Wir haben einen Farbfernseher.**
There are lots of pictures on the wall.	**Es sind viele Bilder an der Wand.**
I haven't got any toothpaste with me.	**Ich habe keine Zahnpasta mit.**
The light is on/off.	**Das Licht ist an/aus.**

HIGHER PHRASES

Should I throw this away?	**Soll ich das wegwerfen?**
It's an electric cooker.	**Es ist ein Elektroherd.**
Is there a socket for a shaver?	**Gibt es eine Steckdose für einen Rasierapparat?**
We've refurnished my room.	**Wir haben mein Zimmer neu möbliert.**

Animals

BASIC VOCABULARY

animal	**das Tier**(e)
pet	**das Haustier**(e)
bird	**der Vogel**(¨)
fish	**der Fisch**(e)
insect	**das Insekt**(en)
goldfish	**der Goldfisch**(e)
hamster	**der Hamster**(-)
guinea pig	**das Meerschwein-chen**(-)
dog	**der Hund**(e)
cat	**die Katze**(n)
mouse	**die Maus**(¨e)
rabbit	**das Kaninchen**(-)
cow	**die Kuh**(¨e)
horse	**das Pferd**(e)
pig	**das Schwein**(e)
sheep	**das Schaf**(e)

HIGHER VOCABULARY

food	**das Futter**
to feed	**füttern**
to eat	**fressen** *(animals only)*
to bark	**bellen**
hut	**die Hütte**(n)
kennel	**die Hundehütte**(n)
cage	**der Käfig**(e)
stable, barn	**der Stall**(¨e)

Are both these signs to be taken seriously?

(HIGHER VOCABULARY)

duck	**die Ente(n)**	fly	**die Fliege(n)**
goose	**die Gans(¨e)**	tortoise	**die Schildkröte(n)**
hen, chicken	**das Huhn(¨er)**	budgie	**der Wellensittich(e)**
cattle	**das Vieh**		

BASIC PHRASES

We don't have any pets.	**Wir haben keine Haustiere.**
I don't like dogs.	**Ich mag Hunde nicht.**
	Ich mag keine Hunde.
My cat is nine months old and is called Tiger.	**Meine Katze ist neun Monate alt und heißt Tiger.**
My rabbit died three years ago.	**Mein Kaninchen ist vor drei Jahren gestorben.**

Doppelsinniges

Die Buchstaben und das Bild gehören zusammen.

Lies beides richtig nacheinander, dann ergibt sich ein neuer Wortsinn. Welcher?

Carl Hagenbecks Tierpark, Telefon 5 40 00 10
2000 Tiere erwarten Sie in einer 75 Jahre alten Parklandschaft. Mehr als 50 Attraktionen. Darüberhinaus: Delphin-, Seelöwen- und Mörderwal-Show im Delphinarium täglich 11.30, 13.30, 15.30 Uhr; Troparium; Dromedar- und Elefantenreiten. Großer Kinderspielplatz. Geöffnet täglich von 8.00 bis 17.30 Uhr. Eintritt Erwachsene 10,50 DM, Kinder (bis 13 Jahre) 5,25 DM. Delphinarium Erwachsene 5,— DM, Kinder 3,50 DM, Troparium Erwachsene 2,— DM, Kinder 1,— DM. U-Bahn-Station Hagenbecks Tierpark.

4 School

School and the school day

school	**die Schule(n)**
to attend	**besuchen**
comprehensive	**die Gesamtschule(n)**
grammar school	**das Gymnasium (Gymnasien)**
secondary modern	**die Hauptschule(n)**
secondary school	**die Realschule(n)**
primary school	**die Grundschule(n)**
nursery	**der Kindergarten(¨)**
building	**das Gebäude(-)**
school yard	**der Schulhof(¨e)**
classroom	**das Klassenzimmer(-)**
library	**die Bibliothek(en)**
pupil	**der Schüler(-)**
teacher	**der Lehrer(-)**
headteacher	**der Direktor(en)**
form teacher	**der Klassenlehrer(-)**
caretaker	**der Hausmeister(-)**
secretary	**der Sekretär(e)**

*NB Feminine forms of the above all add
-in(nen)*

to read	**lesen**
to write	**schreiben**
homework	**die Hausaufgabe(n)**
to learn	**lernen**
to forget	**vergessen**
to study	**studieren**
to ask	**fragen**
to answer	**(be)antworten**
answer	**die Antwort(en)**
to listen	**zuhören** *(sep)*
pen	**der Füller(-)**
biro	**der Kugelschreiber(-),** *coll:* **der Kuli(s)**

pencil	**der Bleistift(e)**
book	**das Buch(¨er)**
exercise book	**das Heft(e)**
paper	**das Papier(e)**
school bag	**die (Schul)mappe(n), die Schultasche(n)**
lesson	**die (Unterrichts)- stunde(n)**
break	**die Pause(n)**
lunchbreak	**die Mittagspause(n)**
to last	**dauern**
school holidays	**die Schulferien** *(pl)*
school trip	**die Klassenfahrt(en)**
exam	**die Prüfung(en), das Examen(-)**
mark	**die Note(n)**
good	**gut**
excellent	**ausgezeichnet**
grade A	**eine Eins** *(approx equivalent)*
a fail (grade)	**eine Fünf(er), eine Sechs(er)**

hall	**die Aula(Aulen)**
laboratory	**das Labor(e)**
language laboratory	**das Sprachlabor(e)**
gymnasium	**die Turnhalle(n)**
staffroom	**das Lehrerzimmer(-)**
workshop	**die Werkstatt(¨en)**
desk	**das Pult(e)**
blackboard	**die Tafel(n)**
board rubber	**der Schwamm(¨e)**
chalk	**die Kreide(n)**

(HIGHER VOCABULARY)

cloth	das Tuch(¨er), *coll:* der Lappen(-)
ruler	das Lineal(e)
eraser, rubber	der Radiergummi(s)
felt-tip pen	der Filzstift(e)
sheet (of paper)	das Blatt(¨er)
piece of paper, note	der Zettel(-)
to cheat	mogeln
to play truant	schwänzen
no school	schulfrei
time off because of heat wave	hitzefrei
to punish	bestrafen
punishment	die Strafe(n), die Strafarbeit(en) *(written piece of work)*
to be in detention	nachsitzen *(sep)*
strict	streng
to be cancelled	ausfallen *(sep)*
to repeat a year	die Klasse/das Jahr wiederholen, sitzenbleiben *(sep)*, durchfallen *(sep)*
to fail (an exam)	nicht bestehen

report	das Zeugnis(se)
fair	befriedigend
satisfactory	ausreichend
poor	mangelhaft
to praise	loben
to promote, move up to a higher class	versetzen
to pass (an exam)	bestehen
written	schriftlich
oral	mündlich
to copy	abschreiben *(sep)*
performance	die Leistung(en)
lesson	der Unterricht *(no pl)*
term	das Semester(-)
register	das Klassenbuch(¨er)
punctual	pünktlich
form captain	der Klassensprecher(-), die Klassensprecherin(nen)
to calculate	rechnen
to discuss	diskutieren
example	das Beispiel(e)
student council	die Schülermitverwaltung(en) (SMV)

BASIC PHRASES

I go to a comprehensive school.	Ich besuche/gehe auf eine Gesamtschule.
The lessons last 40 minutes.	Die Stunden dauern vierzig Minuten.
School finishes at 3.30.	Die Schule ist um halb vier aus.
I get a lot of homework.	Ich habe viele Hausaufgaben.
We take our exams next year.	Wir machen nächstes Jahr unsere Prüfungen.

HIGHER PHRASES

I get on well with my tutor.	Ich komme mit meinem Klassenlehrer gut aus.
We always have Saturdays off.	Samstags ist immer schulfrei.
I hope I'll pass my exams.	Ich hoffe, ich werde meine Examen bestehen.
My report was fairly good.	Mein Zeugnis war befriedigend.
The lesson is cancelled.	Die Stunde fällt aus.

School subjects

BASIC VOCABULARY

timetable	der Stundenplan("e)
subject	das Fach("er)
favourite subject	das Lieblingsfach("er)
interesting	interessant
boring	langweilig
easy	leicht
hard	schwierig
right	richtig
wrong	verkehrt, falsch
language	die Sprache(n)
foreign language	die Fremdsprache(n)
German	Deutsch
French	Französisch
Spanish	Spanisch
English	Englisch
Latin	Latein
expression	der Ausdruck ("e)
science	die Naturwissen-schaft(en)
physics	die Physik
chemistry	die Chemie
biology	die Biologie
maths	die Mathematik, coll: Mathe
computer studies	die Informatik

computer	der Computer(-)
history	die Geschichte
geography	die Geographie, die Erdkunde
music	die Musik
religious education	die Religion
art	die Kunst
handicraft	das Werken
woodwork	die Holzarbeit
metalwork	die Metallarbeit
technical drawing	technisches Zeichnen
technology	die Technik
cookery	das Kochen
needlework	die Handarbeit
typewriting	das Maschinen-schreiben
sport	der Sport
gymnastics	das Turnen
sport & gymnastics	der Sportunterricht

HIGHER VOCABULARY

compulsory subject	das Pflichtfach("er)
option	das Wahlfach("er)

BASIC PHRASES

I like learning German.	Ich lerne gern Deutsch.
I prefer studying maths.	Ich ziehe Mathe vor. Ich lerne lieber Mathe.
I find physics hard.	Ich finde Physik schwierig.
I have to work hard in history.	Für Geschichte muß ich viel arbeiten.
I'm not very good at biology.	Ich bin nicht sehr gut in Biologie.

GYMNASIUM NEU·ULM
(Neuspr. Gymn.; Math.-nat. Gymn. i. A.)

JAHRESZEUGNIS

Maria BAGEHORN

geboren am **8. Oktober** 19**69** in *Memmingen*

Kreis —————————— *cv.* Bekenntnisses,

hat im Schuljahr 19**85/86** die Klasse **10b** des neuspr. Gymnasiums besucht.

Betragen und Fleiß der Schülerin verdienen Anerkennung.

LEISTUNGEN:

Religionslehre	*sehr gut*	Gemeinschaftskunde	
Deutsch	*gut*	Geschichte	*gut*
Latein	*ausreichend*	Erdkunde	—
(1. Fremdsprache)		Sozialkunde	*gut*
Englisch	*gut*		
(2. Fremdsprache)		Kunsterziehung	*befriedigend*
Französisch	*gut*		
(3. Fremdsprache)		Musik	*gut*
Mathematik	*ausreichend*		
		Leibeserziehung	*sehr gut*
Naturwissenschaften			
Physik	*mangelhaft*	—	—
Chemie	—	—	—
Biologie	*gut*		

Am Wahlunterricht in Italienisch hat sie mit Erfolg teilgenommen.

Di**e** Schüler**in** ist damit zum Eintritt in die Oberstufe eines Gymnasiums berechtigt (Oberstufenreife).

Neu-Ulm, den **23**. Juli 19**86**

DER DIREKTOR: DER KLASSLEITER:

Schnebel

Notenstufen: sehr gut, gut, befriedigend, ausreichend, mangelhaft, ungenügend.

J. Maiß, München

In which subjects has this pupil done extremely well?

30

HIGHER PHRASES

I'm doing art as an option.	Ich mache Kunst als Wahlfach.
My favourite subject is science.	Meine Lieblingsfächer sind die
is science.	Naturwissenschaften.

Plans for the future

HIGHER VOCABULARY

A level		student	der Student(en)
(approx equivalent)	das Abitur		die Studentin(nen)
O level		university	die Universität(en),
(approx equivalent)	die Realschulreife,		*coll:* die Uni(s)
	die Mittlere Reife	future	die Zukunft
sixth form		past	die Vergangenheit
(approx equivalent)	die Oberstufe(n)	to prepare oneself for	sich vorbereiten auf
technical college	die Berufsschule(n)		(+ *acc*)
college	die Fachhochschule(n)	experience	die Erfahrung(en)
careers guidance	die Berufsberatung(en)	experienced	erfahren
apprentice	der Lehrling(e)	to decide	beschließen,
apprenticeship	die Lehre(n)		sich entscheiden
course	der Kurs(e)		

HIGHER PHRASES

I'd like to become an engineer.	Ich möchte Ingenieur werden.
I hope to go to university.	Ich hoffe, zur Uni zu gehen.
I want to stay on at school.	Ich möchte auf der Schule bleiben.
I haven't got any definite plans.	Ich habe noch keine festen Pläne.
I intend leaving school this year.	Ich habe vor, die Schule dieses Jahr zu verlassen.

5 Free time and entertainment

Leisure time and hobbies

BASIC VOCABULARY

hobby	**das Hobby(s)**
free time, leisure (time)	**die Freizeit**
interest	**das Interesse(n)**
to begin	**anfangen** (*sep*), **beginnen**
to stop	**aufhören** (*sep*)
outing, excursion	**der Ausflug("e)**, **die Fahrt(en)**
round trip	**die Rundfahrt(en)**
to go out	**ausgehen** (*sep*)
to drive, travel	**fahren**
visit	**der Besuch(e)**
to view	**besichtigen**
to photograph, take a picture of	**fotografieren**, *coll:* **knipsen**
camera	**der Fotoapparat(e)**
picture (photograph)	**das Foto(s)**
to look	**schauen**, *coll:* **gucken**
to meet	**(sich) treffen** (*mit* + *dat*)
to collect	**sammeln**
stamp	**die Briefmarke(n)**
coin	**die Münze(n)**
programme	**das Programm(e)**
card	**die Karte(n)**
to stick	**kleben**
music	**die Musik**
orchestra	**das Orchester(-)**
instrument	**das Instrument(e)**
flute	**die Flöte(n)**
recorder	**die Blockflöte(n)**
violin	**die Geige(n)**
guitar	**die Gitarre(n)**
piano	**das Klavier(e)**
drum	**das Schlagzeug(e)**
trumpet	**die Trompete(n)**
classical	**klassisch**
pop music	**die Popmusik**
hit	**der Hit(s)**, **der Schlager(-)**
hit parade, charts	**die Hitparade(n)**
group	**die Gruppe(n)**
singer	**der Sänger(-)**, **die Sängerin(nen)**
to listen	**(zu)hören** (*sep*)
programme	**die Sendung(en)**
radio	**das Radio(s)**
record	**die (Schall)platte(n)**
single	**die Single(s)**
LP	**die Langspielplatte(n)**, **die LP(s)**
record player	**der Plattenspieler(-)**
cassette	**die Kassette(n)**
cassette recorder	**der Kassetten-rekorder(-)**
loud	**laut**
quiet	**leise**
to watch TV	**fernsehen** (*sep*)
on TV	**im Fernsehen**
computer	**der Computer(-)**
to read	**lesen**
newspaper	**die Zeitung(en)**
to sit down	**sich hinsetzen** (*sep*)
to lie down	**sich hinlegen** (*sep*)

(BASIC VOCABULARY)

magazine	die Zeitschrift(en),
	das Magazin(e),
	die Illustrierte(n)
youth club	der Jugendklub(s)

HIGHER VOCABULARY

leisure activity	die Freizeitbeschäftigung(en)
collection	die Sammlung(en)
member	das Mitglied(er)
boy scout	der Pfadfinder(-)
girl guide	die Pfadfinderin(nen)
to enquire	sich erkundigen
to take part (in)	teilnehmen an (sep) (+dat)
outdoors	im Freien
exhibition	die Ausstellung(en)
guided tour	die Führung(en)
guide book	der Reiseführer(-)
courier	der Reiseleiter(-)
sight	die Sehenswürdigkeit(en)
tape	das Band(¨er)
tape recorder	das Tonbandgerät(e)

radio	der Rundfunk
news	die Nachrichten (pl)
announcer	der Ansager(-),
	die Ansagerin(nen)
to transmit, broadcast	senden
episode	die Folge(n), der Teil(e)
series	die Sendereihe(n), die Serie(n)
paperback	das Taschenbuch(¨er)
novel	der Roman(e)
sticker	der Aufkleber(-)
photo	die Aufnahme(n)
slide	das Dia(s)
to draw	zeichnen
to paint	malen
to make things with your hands	basteln
to knit	stricken
to crochet	häkeln
to sew	nähen
chess	(das) Schach(spiel)
to play chess	Schach spielen
band	die Kapelle(n)
brass band	die Blaskapelle(n)

BASIC PHRASES

My hobbies are music and football.	Meine Hobbys sind Musik und Fußball.
I like reading magazines.	Ich lese gern Zeitschriften.
I am interested in pop music.	Ich interessiere mich für Popmusik.
I often meet my friends in town.	Ich treffe mich oft mit meinen Freunden in der Stadt.
Piano-playing is fun.	Klavierspielen macht Spaß.

HIGHER PHRASES

I like being outdoors.	Ich bin gern im Freien.
I'm a member of a band.	Ich bin Mitglied einer Kapelle. / Ich spiele in einer Kapelle mit.
I visited an art exhibition.	Ich habe eine Kunstausstellung besichtigt.
I used to be a scout.	Ich war früher Pfadfinder.
My favourite series is "Neighbours".	Meine Lieblingsserie ist „Neighbours".

What are these TV programmes?

Heute vormittag

Ab 12.00 nur über ARD
10.00 heute; **10.03** Sportschau;
10.55 Der Ruf des Herzens Nachbarn (Vom 30. 11. 1988); **11.40** Ze-
le-Zoo; **12.10** Plusminus; **12.55**
Presseschau; **13.00** heute

1. Programm

13.15 Vorschau auf das
ARD-Programm der Woche
13.45 Nachbarn
Skizzen aus Mittel-
und Osteuropa
14.30 Für Kinder
Flickerl und Fleckerl
Harrah! Ich hab' den Dieb
15.00 Formel Eins (Stereo)
Die ARD-Hitparade
mit Kai Böcking
15.45 Roger Rabbit und die
Geheimnisse von Toon-Stadt
Blick hinter die Kinokulissen
mit Joanna Cassidy
16.35 Musikalischer Advents-
kalender (Stereo)
Eine Sendung mit Advents-
und Weihnachtsliedern
Dargeboten von René Kollo
und Gästen
René Kollo begrüßt in der
Saarbrücker Saarlandhalle
bekannte Gäste, wie zum
Donath, Lolita,

2. Programm

9.30 ZDF — Ihr Programm (Stereo)
10.00 Mit Vorschau
auf die kommende Woche
12.10 Nachbarn in Europa
Internationales Magazin am
Wochenende
Im Studio: Elettra de Salvo'
13.40 Diese Woche
14.00 Afrikanische Wurzeln
1. Das Niltal —
Quelle der Kulturen
Von Gaston Bart-Williams
14.30 Wir stellen uns
ZDF-Chefredakteur
Klaus Breser im Gespräch mit
Zuschauern zum Thema
,,Wie soll das Fernsehen
informieren?''
Moderation: Frank Elstner
15.15 Faszination Musik
16.05 Auf einem langen Weg
Wie die Adameks zu Fuß nach
Westen wandern
Nach dem gleichnamigen Ro-
man von Gudrun Pausewang

Sports

BASIC VOCABULARY

sport	**der Sport** (Sportarten)	swimming costume	**der Badeanzug("e)**
to do sport	**Sport treiben**	swimming trunks	**die Badehose(n)**
sports ground	**der Sportplatz("e)**	swimming cap	**die Bademütze(n)**
stadium	**das Stadion(Stadien)**	swimming-pool	**das Schwimmbad("er)**
to play	**spielen**	open-air pool	**das Freibad("er)**
club	**der Verein(e),**	indoor pool	**das Hallenbad("er)**
	der Klub(s)	towel	**das Handtuch("er),**
team	**die Mannschaft(en)**		**das Badetuch("er)**
final	**das Endspiel(e)**	waterpolo	**das Wasserball**
fan	**der Fan(s)**	to jump	**springen**
to win	**gewinnen**	to throw	**werfen**
to lose	**verlieren**	windsurfing	**das Windsurfen**
		boat	**das Boot(e)**
to fish	**angeln**		
to swim	**schwimmen**	ball	**der Ball("e)**
to bathe	**baden**	football	**der Fußball("e)**

(BASIC VOCABULARY)

handball	**der Handball("e)**
shuttlecock	**der Federball("e)**
volleyball	**der Volleyball("e)**
basketball	**der Basketball("e)**
badminton	**das Badminton**
tennis	**das Tennis**
table tennis	**das Tischtennis**
beginner	**der Anfänger(-),**
	die Anfängerin(nen)
hike	**die Wanderung(en)**
to hike	**wandern**
to walk	**spazierengehen** (*sep*)
walk	**der Spaziergang("e)**
rucksack	**der Rucksack("e)**
sign	**das Schild(er)**
to run	**laufen, rennen**
jogging	**das Jogging**
to jog	**joggen**
to ride	**reiten**
to cycle	**radfahren** (*sep*)
to ski	**skilaufen** (*sep*),
	skifahren (*sep*)
ski	**der Ski(er)**
skilift	**der Skilift(e)**
skistick	**der Skistock("e)**

HIGHER VOCABULARY

to practise	**üben**
to train	**trainieren**
tracksuit	**der Trainingsanzug("e)**
to get fit	**sich trimmen**
point	**der Punkt(e)**

goal	**das Tor(e)**
amateur	**der Amateur(e)**
professional	**der Profi(s)**
cup	**der Pokal(e)**
world cup	**die Weltmeister-**
	schaft(en)
first division	
(*W. German football*)	**die Bundesliga**
result	**das Ergebnis(se)**
changing room	**der Umkleideraum("e)**
racket, bat	**der Schläger(-)**
to catch	**fangen**
to shoot	**schießen**
net	**das Netz(e)**
to play skittles	**kegeln**
athletics	**die Leichtathletik**
to dive	**tauchen**
to sail	**segeln**
sailing boat	**das Segelboot(e)**
to row	**rudern**
rowing boat	**das Ruderboot**
fishing rod	**die Angelrute(n)**
to climb	**klettern**
cable car	
(*at a ski resort*)	**die Seilbahn(en)**
signpost	**der Wegweiser(-)**
rollerskates	**die Rollschuhe** (*pl*)
to rollerskate	**rollschuhlaufen** (*sep*)
ice skates	**die Schlittschuhe** (*pl*)
to ice skate	**schlittschuhlaufen** (*sep*)
hunt	**die Jagd**

BASIC PHRASES

I like swimming.	**Ich schwimme gern.**
Do you play tennis as well?	**Spielst du auch Tennis?**
I play for the school team.	**Ich spiele in der Schulmannschaft.**
I don't do a lot of sport.	**Ich treibe nicht viel Sport.**
I saw the match on TV.	**Ich habe das Spiel im Fernsehen gesehen.**

35

HIGHER PHRASES

They won 1–0.	**Sie haben eins zu null gewonnen.**
The game was a draw.	**Das Spiel endete unentschieden.**
I'd like to hire a rowing boat.	**Ich möchte gern ein Ruderboot mieten.**
I train three times a week.	**Ich trainiere dreimal die Woche.**
I jog to keep fit.	**Ich jogge, um fit zu bleiben.**

radfahren und schwimmen

Sports headlines from newspapers

Berichte aus dem Regionalsport

Ein Tiroler verhalf Tamara zum ersten Weltmeistertitel

Spiel auf ein Tor ohne Tor

Werder zu ideenlos / Hamburger Ersatzmann Thomforde Mann des Tages

Entertainment

BASIC VOCABULARY

entrance	**der Eingang(¨e)**	group	**die Gruppe(n)**
entry	**der Eintritt**	singer	**der Sänger(-),**
entrance fee	**das Eintrittsgeld(er)**		**die Sängerin(nen)**
ticket	**die Karte(n)**	to sing	**singen**
box office, cash desk	**die Kasse(n)**	song	**das Lied(er)**
exit	**der Ausgang(¨e)**	to dance	**tanzen**
emergency exit	**der Notausgang(¨e)**	(youth) club	**der (Jugend)klub(s)**
museum	**das Museum(Museen)**	cinema	**das Kino(s)**
(medieval) castle	**die Burg(en)**	film	**der Film(e)**
castle	**das Schloß(¨sser)**	documentary	**der Dokumentar-**
zoo	**der Zoo(s),**		**film(e)**
	der Tiergarten(¨)	thriller	**der Krimi(s)**
		cartoon	**der Trickfilm(e)**
disco	**die Disko(thek)(en)**	western	**der Wildwestfilm(e),**
concert	**das Konzert(e)**		**der Western(-)**

(BASIC VOCABULARY)

performance, showing	**die Vorstellung(en)**	to finish	**zu Ende sein**
seat	**der Platz(¨e)**	fair	**der Jahrmarkt(¨e),**
available, free	**frei**		**die Kirmes** (*no pl*)
		circus	**der Zirkus(se)**
theatre	**das Theater(-)**	monkey	**der Affe(n)**
play	**das Theaterstück(e),**	elephant	**der Elefant(en)**
	das Schauspiel(e),	lion	**der Löwe(n)**
	das Drama(Dramen)	snake	**die Schlange(n)**
circle	**der Rang(¨e)**	tiger	**der Tiger(-)**
row	**die Reihe(n)**		

16

Freitag

Studio
17.30 Zwei Welten
20.00 Das Leben ist ein
langer ruhiger Fluß
21.45 Bird
Casablanca
18.00 Das Leben ist ein
langer ruhiger Fluß
19.30 Im Jahr der Schildkröte
21.00 Brennende Betten
23.15 Red Heat

Kino

DÜSSELDORF
Bambi
18.00/20.00 Jane B.
22.30 Out of Rosenheim
(Hauptprogramm erfragen
unter 353635)
Souterrain
18.00 Garp und wie er die
Welt sah
21.00 Maria & Josef
22.45 Casablanca
Metropol
19.30 West Side Story
22.15 Das Leben des Brian +
Der Sinn des Lebens
Cinema
23.59 Little Shop of Horrors
(Hauptprogramm erfragen
unter 131374)
HILDEN
Der Bahnhof
20.15/22.30 Harold and
Maude
NEUSS
Hitch
18.00 Pink Floyd: The Wall
20.15 The Untouchables
22.30 Blues Brothers
RATINGEN
Autokino Minidomm
20.00 Willow
22.00 Die Geister, die ich rief
24.00 Die Nackte Zelle
SOLINGEN
Der Keller
18.45/23.00 Die Beduinen
von Paris
21.00 Zwei Welten
WUPPERTAL
Cinema
16.00/17.45 Harold & Maude
19.30 Die letzte Versuchung
Christi
22.45 Betty Blue - 37.2
am Morgen + Storm

Musik

BOCHUM
Steel Pulse
20.00 Zeche (Halle)
Gefährliche Welle Disco
22.00 Zeche (Halle)
DORTMUND
Bon Jovi
20.00 Westfalenhalle
2 Jahre Live-Station - mit:
Sambaia (und Buffet etc.)
21.00 Live-Station
DUISBURG
The Blues Brothers Revival
Band
20.00 Ratskeller Hamborn
DÜSSELDORF
Benefiz-Rockkonzert: Peter-
Zerbe-Band / Sitte / Breez
19.30 Freizeitstätte Garath
Cliff Barnes and the Fear
of Winning
20.00 Spektakulum
Düsseldorfer Symphoniker -
Werke von Ligeti, Hummel,
Dvorak (Ltg.: Muhai Tang)
20.00 Tonhalle
Werner Lämmerhirt (Gitarre)
21.00 Delifrance
Gene Connors Band
21.00 Timp
Stetson Power (Speed-
country & Kittypop)
21.30 Haus Holland (Selbst-
verw. Wohnprojekt)
Gangster of Love
(Rhythm'n and Blues)
21.30 bel etage
KREFELD
Königsburg-Geburtstag
a. mit Weltstar Gloria
20.00 Königsburg
KÖLN
Sanfte Liebe
tern), Jinx
Paint The T
cial Guest
19.00 (Gr.
Kr

AL CAPONE.
Er beherrschte Chicago mit absoluter Macht. Keiner konnte ihn aufhalten.

Bis Eliot Ness
und seine Männer sich schworen, ihn zu vernichten.

THE
UNTOUCHABLES
-DIE UNBESTECHLICHEN-

PARAMOUNT PICTURES PRÄSENTIERT EINE ART LINSON PRODUCTION · EIN BRIAN DE PALMA FILM
THE UNTOUCHABLES · KEVIN COSTNER · CHARLES MARTIN SMITH · ANDY GARCIA
als AL CAPONE und   als MALONE
Musik ENNIO MORRICONE · Visual Consultant PATRIZIA VON BRANDENSTEIN · Schnitt JERRY GREENBERG
Art Director WILLIAM A. ELLIOTT · Kamera STEPHEN H. BURUM, A.S.C.
Drehbuch DAVID MAMET · Produktion ART LINSON · Regie BRIAN DE PALMA · EIN PARAMOUNT FILM IM VERLEIH DER

AB 15. OKTOBER IM KINO

HIGHER VOCABULARY

performance	die Aufführung(en)		stage	die Bühne(n)
queue	die Schlange(n)		stalls	das Parkett
to queue up	Schlange stehen		hall	der Saal(Säle)
sold out	ausverkauft		actor	der Schauspieler(-)
famous	berühmt		comedy	die Komödie(n)
cloakroom	die Garderobe(n)		to decide	beschließen
balcony	der Balkon(e)		to obtain, get	besorgen

BASIC PHRASES

I went to a concert last night.	Ich war gestern abend im Konzert.
How much are seats in the circle?	Was kosten die Plätze im ersten Rang?
I'd like two tickets at 5 marks.	Ich möchte zwei Karten zu fünf Mark.
Is the castle closed today?	Ist das Schloß heute zu?
Do you want to go to the cinema?	Hast du Lust, ins Kino zu gehen?

HIGHER PHRASES

Please reserve a ticket for me for Saturday.	Bitte legen Sie mir eine Karte für Samstag zurück.
Where could I get the tickets?	Wo könnte ich die Karten besorgen?
People were queuing up.	Die Leute standen Schlange.
What about a play?	Wie wäre es mit einem Schauspiel?
Unfortunately the performance is sold out.	Leider ist die Vorstellung ausverkauft.

Opinions

BASIC VOCABULARY

good	gut		particularly	besonders
interesting	interessant		quite	ganz
funny	komisch, lustig		really	wirklich
great	großartig, toll,		not at all	gar nicht
	coll: prima, klasse			
rubbish	(der) Quatsch		to think	denken
awful	furchtbar, schrecklich		to believe	glauben, meinen
boring	langweilig		to find	finden
silly	dumm,		to enjoy	gefallen
	coll: doof, blöd		to like	mögen
			to hope	hoffen
very	sehr			
fairly	ziemlich			

HIGHER VOCABULARY

success	**der Erfolg**(e)
exciting	**spannend**
excellent	**ausgezeichnet,**
	coll: **Spitze**
popular	**beliebt**
nonsense	**der Blödsinn**

to advise	**raten**
to recommend	**empfehlen**
to suggest	**vorschlagen** (*sep*)
to prefer	**vorziehen** (*sep*)

BASIC PHRASES

The film was really great.	**Der Film war wirklich toll.**
I enjoyed it a lot.	**Es hat mir gut gefallen.**
I think it is very funny.	**Ich finde, es ist sehr komisch.**
I'm not interested in that.	**Das interessiert mich nicht.**
That was rubbish!	**Das war Quatsch!**

HIGHER PHRASES

I don't think much of this musuem.	**Ich halte nicht viel von diesem Museum.**
What do you dislike on TV?	**Was siehst du im Fernsehen nicht gern?**
What did you think of the concert?	**Wie fandest du das Konzert?**
I prefer comedies.	**Ich ziehe Komödien vor. / Ich mag Komödien lieber.**
I can recommend this book.	**Dieses Buch kann ich wirklich empfehlen.**

EVITA

„Don't Cry For Me, Argentina!"

Der Musical-Welterfolg endlich im Original

Eines der größten Musical-Erfolge des Erfolgsteams Andrew Lloyd-Webber und Tim Rice. Evita, 1980 als

Meilenstein des Musical-Theaters der 80er Jahre gefeiert, kommt in original Broadway-Version.

Triumph für Dustin Hoffman:

Der „Goldene Bär" für Hollywoods Kassenknüller

„Rain Man" gewann bei den Berliner Filmfestspielen

Berlin (dpa). Die USA sind bei den die beste Regie aufgenommen, der

39

6 Work

Jobs

work	**die Arbeit**	driver	**der Fahrer(-)**
worker, labourer	**der Arbeiter(-)**	bus driver	**der Busfahrer(-)**
job	**der Job(s), die Stelle(n)**	lorry driver	**der LKW-Fahrer(-)**
profession	**der Beruf(e)**	pilot	**der Pilot(en)**
boss	**der Chef(s)**	stewardess	**die Stewardeß(ssen)**
industry	**die Industrie(n)**	builder	**der Bauarbeiter(-)**
factory	**die Fabrik(en)**	mechanic	**der Mechaniker(-)**
shopkeeper, grocer	**der Kaufmann(Kaufleute)**	farmer	**der Bauer(n)**
shop	**das Geschäft(e)**	postman	**der Briefträger(-)**
		electrician	**der Elektriker(-)**
chemist	**der Drogist(en),**	policeman	**der Polizist(en)**
	der Apotheker(-)		
doctor	**der Arzt(¨e)**	office	**das Büro(s)**
dentist	**der Zahnarzt(¨e)**	secretary	**der Sekretär(e)**
nurse (female)	**die Kranken-**	teacher	**der Lehrer(-)**
	schwester(n)	headteacher	**der Direktor(en)**
nurse (male)	**der Krankenpfleger(-)**	official	**der Beamte(n)**
		musician	**der Musiker(-)**
baker	**der Bäcker(-)**	cook	**der Koch(¨e)**
butcher	**der Metzger(-),**	waiter	**der Kellner(-)**
	der Fleischer(-)	chambermaid	**das Zimmer-**
barber	**der Friseur(e)**		**mädchen(-)**

NB Feminine forms of the above all add -in(nen), except: **die Kauffrau(en), die Ärztin, die Zahnärztin, die Friseuse(n), die Bäuerin, die Beamtin, die Köchin**

		firm	**die Firma(Firmen)**
employee	**der/die Angestellte(n),**	factory	**das Werk(e)**
	der Arbeitnehmer(-)	wage	**der Lohn(¨e)**
job centre	**das Arbeitsamt(¨er)**	salary	**das Gehalt(¨er)**
unemployed	**arbeitslos**	end of day's work	**der Feierabend(e)**
to be on the dole	**arbeitslos sein,**	advertising	**die Werbung(en)**
	coll: **stempeln gehen**		
employed	**berufstätig**	fireman	**der Feuerwehr-**
self-employed	**selbständig**		**mann(¨er)**
business	**der Betrieb(e)**	soldier	**der Soldat(en)**

(HIGHER VOCABULARY)

sailor	der Matrose(n)	expert	der Fachmann("er)
salesman	der Verkäufer(-)	vet	der Tierarzt("e)
businessman	der Geschäfts-	actor	der Schauspieler(-)
	mann("er)	referee	der Schiedsrichter(-)
engineer	der Ingenieur(e)	cashier	der Kassierer(-)
conductor (transport)	der Schaffner(-)	interpreter	der Dolmetscher(-)

NB Feminine forms of the above all add -in(nen), except: **die Feuerwehrfrau(en), die Matrosin, die Geschäftsfrau(en) die Fachfrau(en), die Tierärztin**

BASIC PHRASES

My father is a teacher.	**Mein Vater ist Lehrer.**
My mother works for Kodak.	**Meine Mutter arbeitet bei Kodak.**
My sister is a secretary.	**Meine Schwester ist Sekretärin.**
My father has his own shop.	**Mein Vater hat sein eigenes Geschäft.**

HIGHER PHRASES

He finishes work at five o'clock.	**Er hat um fünf Uhr Feierabend.**
I'd like to become an engineer.	**Ich möchte Ingenieur werden.**
I was at the job centre yesterday.	**Gestern war ich auf dem Arbeitsamt.**

What jobs are being advertised?

41

Spare-time jobs and pocket money

BASIC VOCABULARY

to work (do casual work)	**arbeiten, jobben**
pocket money	**das Taschengeld** *(no pl)*
pound	**das Pfund** *(Sterling)* *(no pl)*
to babysit	**babysitten**
bank	**die Bank(en),**
	die Sparkasse(n)
bank note	**die Banknote(n)**
cheque book	**das Scheckbuch("er)**
to save	**sparen für** *(+ acc)*
to earn	**verdienen**
to get	**bekommen,**
	coll: **kriegen**
to cost	**kosten**

to buy	**kaufen**
expensive	**teuer**
cheap	**billig**
free	**kostenlos**
a lot	**viel**
a little	**wenig**

HIGHER VOCABULARY

to spend	**ausgeben** *(sep)*
to lend	**leihen**
to belong	**gehören**
to cash (cheque)	**einlösen** *(sep)*
account	**das Konto (Konten)**

BASIC PHRASES

I work every Saturday.	**Ich arbeite / jobbe jeden Samstag.**
I earn £2 an hour.	**Ich verdiene zwei Pfund pro Stunde.**
I'm saving up for a car.	**Ich spare für ein Auto.**
I get very little pocket money.	**Ich kriege sehr wenig Taschengeld.**

HIGHER PHRASES

I pay the money into my account.	**Ich zahle das Geld auf mein Konto ein.**
I spend all my money.	**Ich gebe all mein Geld aus.**

Wenn du etwas kaufst, was ist für dich wichtig?

Wichtig für mich ist . . .	Gesamt	Männlich	Weiblich
. . . daß es modisch ist und dem neuesten Trend entspricht	11,4	10,7	11,7
. . . daß es meinem persönlichen Stil entspricht	75,2	69,4	80,7
daß es eine teure Marke ist, die auffällt	3,0	3,2	2,8

Wichtig für mich ist . . .	Gesamt	Männlich	Weiblich
. . . daß ich überlegt kaufe, Preise und Qualität vergleiche	45,5	46,2	45,3
. . . nichts zu kaufen, was gesundheits- oder umweltschädlich ist	32,1	29,8	34,6
. . . keine Produkte aus politisch umstrittenen Ländern zu kaufen	11,3	10,1	12,6

Alle Angaben in Prozent

7 Travel and transport

Finding the way

map	die (Land)karte(n)
plan	der Stadtplan(¨e)
to be a stranger	fremd sein
way	der Weg(e)
direction	die Richtung(en)
to follow	folgen
to take	nehmen
along	entlang
opposite	gegenüber
near	neben, in der Nähe von
behind	hinter
in front of	vor
over	über
not far from	nicht weit von
to	zu
past	an . . . vorbei
up	hinauf
over	hinüber
over there	da drüben
down	hinunter
here	hier
nearest	nächst
to look for	suchen
at the end	am Ende
there	da, dort

left	links
right	rechts
straight on	geradeaus
as far as	bis zu
first, second	erste, zweite
immediately	gleich, sofort
wide	breit
narrow	eng
corner	die Ecke(n)
square	der Platz(¨e)
side	die Seite(n)
on foot	zu Fuß
pedestrian	der Fußgänger(-)

side road	die Nebenstraße(n), die Querstraße(n)
to find out, make enquiries	sich erkundigen
to get lost	sich verlaufen (on foot), sich verfahren (in car), sich verirren (both)
to cross	überqueren
to turn	abbiegen (sep)

How do I get to the station?	Wie komme ich zum Bahnhof?
Where's the nearest bank?	Wo ist die nächste Bank?
I'm a stranger here too.	Ich bin hier auch fremd.
Take the third road on the left.	Nehmen Sie die dritte Straße links.
I'm looking for a hotel around here.	Ich suche ein Hotel in der Nähe.

HIGHER PHRASES

Turn left at the town hall.	**Biegen Sie am Rathaus links ab.**
Cross the bridge.	**Überqueren Sie die Brücke.**
I have got lost.	**Ich habe mich verirrt.**
Where can I find out?	**Wo kann ich mich erkundigen?**

What do these signs mean?

Public transport

BASIC VOCABULARY

to travel	**fahren, reisen**
ticket	**die Fahrkarte(n),**
	der Fahrschein(e)
single	**einfach**
return	**hin und zurück**
return ticket	**die Rückfahrkarte(n)**
ticket machine	**der Fahrkarten-**
	automat(en)
to set off	**abfahren** (*sep*)
departure	**die Abfahrt(en)**
driver	**der Fahrer(-)**
passenger	**der Fahrgast("e),**
	der Passagier(e)
timetable	**der Fahrplan("e)**
journey	**die Fahrt(en),**
	die Reise(n)
luggage	**das Gepäck** (*no pl*)
suitcase	**der Koffer(-)**

to arrive	**ankommen** (*sep*)
arrival	**die Ankunft("e)**
to get out	**aussteigen** (*sep*)
to get on	**einsteigen** (*sep*)
exit	**der Ausgang("e)**
entrance	**der Eingang("e)**
waiting-room	**der Warteraum("e),**
	der Wartesaal(säle)
quick	**schnell**
slow	**langsam**
early	**früh**
late	**spät**
on time	**pünktlich**
airport	**der Flughafen(")**
aeroplane	**das Flugzeug(e)**
aircraft	**die Maschine(n)**

(BASIC VOCABULARY)

luggage trolley	der Kofferkuli(s)
to fly	fliegen
to fly off, leave	abfliegen (sep)
to take off	starten
to land	landen

port, harbour	der Hafen(¨)
boat	das Boot(e)
ship	das Schiff(e)
steamer	der Dampfer(-)
crossing	die Überfahrt(en)
seasick	seekrank

railway	die (Eisen)bahn(en)
German Railways	die Deutsche Bundesbahn (DB)
station	der Bahnhof(¨e)
main station	der Hauptbahnhof(¨e)
platform	der Bahnsteig(e)
tram	die Straßenbahn(en)
underground	die U-Bahn(en)
underground station	der U-Bahnhof(¨e)
train	der Zug(¨e)
city commuter train	die S-Bahn(en)
local train	der Nahverkehrszug(¨e)
fast non-stop train	der D-Zug(¨e)
fast 'stopping' train	der Eilzug(¨e)
intercity	der Intercityzug(¨e)
Trans-Europe Express	der TEE-Zug(¨e)

track	das Gleis(e)
carriage	der Wagen(-)
dining car	der Speisewagen(-)
smoker	der Raucher(-)
non-smoker	der Nichtraucher(-)
to catch	erreichen, coll: kriegen
direct	direkt
to change	umsteigen (sep)
to book	buchen
to reserve	reservieren
to stamp (ticket)	entwerten
ticket office	der Schalter(-)

lost property office	das Fundbüro(s)
information	die Auskunft(¨e)
to pay	zahlen
supplement	der Zuschlag(¨e)
first class	erste Klasse
second class	zweite Klasse

bus	der Bus(se)
bus stop	die Bushaltestelle(n)
bus station	der Busbahnhof(¨e)
to hold tight	sich festhalten (sep)
at the front	vorne
at the back	hinten
in the middle	mitten, in der Mitte

via	über
weekdays	werktags, wochentags
to leave	verlassen
taxi	das Taxi(s)
to take	nehmen
to call	rufen, aufrufen (sep)

HIGHER VOCABULARY

flight	der Flug(¨e)
return flight	der Rückflug(¨e)
departure time	die Abflugzeit(en)
seat belt	der Sicherheitsgurt(e)
to fasten one's seat belt	sich anschnallen (sep)
check-in	die Gepäckannahme(n)
baggage reclaim	die Gepäckausgabe(n)
stewardess	die Stewardeß(ssen)
helicopter	der Hubschrauber(-)
connection	die Verbindung(en)

single ticket	die Einzelkarte(n)
ticket valid for several journeys	die Mehrfahrtenkarte(n)
student ticket	die Schülerfahrkarte(n)
travel card	die Netzkarte(n)
to buy a ticket	eine Fahrkarte lösen
available	erhältlich
cost (of ticket)	der Fahrpreis(e)
valid	gültig

To which form of public transport do these signs apply?

B

H Bahnbus Europabus

Deutsche Bundesbahn

DB FAHRKARTEN
—NAHVERKEHR—

● Moderne Automaten

● für Fahrausweise bis 50 km

● in der Schalterhalle

Bitte, nutzen Sie den Vorteil rascher Selbstbedienung

DB

(HIGHER VOCABULARY)

supplement payable	**zuschlagspflichtig**
seat reservation	**die Platzkarte(n)**
to travel without paying	**schwarzfahren** (*sep*)
compartment	**das Abteil(e)**
luggage rack	**das Gepäcknetz(e)**
to lean out	**(sich) hinauslehnen** (*sep*)
to inspect (tickets)	**kontrollieren**
ticket inspector	**der Schaffner(-),**
	der Kontrolleur(e)
got on (at last stop)	**zugestiegen**
couchette	**der Liegewagen(-)**
sleeping-car	**der Schlafwagen(-)**
scheduled	**planmäßig**
late, delayed	**verspätet**
delay	**die Verspätung(en)**

luggage locker	**das Schließfach(¨er)**
left luggage office	**die Gepäckauf-**
	bewahrung(en)
to run	**verkehren**
to miss	**verpassen**
to go away	**verreisen**
travel agent's	**das Reisebüro(s)**
to last	**dauern**
hovercraft	**das Luftkissenboot(e)**
ferry	**die Fähre(n)**
car ferry	**die Autofähre(n)**
on board	**an Bord**
line, company	**die Linie(n)**
meeting point	**der Treffpunkt(e)**
bank holiday	**der Feiertag(e)**

BASIC PHRASES

Two return tickets to Bonn.	**Zweimal hin und zurück nach Bonn.**
Does the tram go there?	**Fährt die Straßenbahn dorthin?**
Do I have to change?	**Muß ich umsteigen?**
Which bus goes to Kassel?	**Welcher Bus fährt nach Kassel?**
Which platform does the train go from?	**Von welchem Gleis fährt der Zug ab?**

HIGHER PHRASES

Is there a train connection?	**Gibt es eine Bahnverbindung?**
Can you get a ticket on the train?	**Kann man die Fahrkarte im Zug lösen?**
Can you confirm my return flight?	**Können Sie meinen Rückflug bestätigen?**
The train was delayed.	**Der Zug hatte Verspätung.**
I've missed the ferry.	**Ich habe die Fähre verpaßt.**

Private transport

BASIC VOCABULARY

bicycle	**das (Fahr)rad(¨er)**
cyclist	**der (Fahr) radfahrer(·)**
scooter	**das Mofa(s)**
motorbike	**das Motorrad(¨er),**

car	**das Auto(s),**
	der Wagen(-),
	der PKW(s)
lorry	**der LKW(s)**

(BASIC VOCABULARY)

front wheel	das Vorderrad(¨er)
back wheel	das Hinterrad(¨er)
tyre	der Reifen(-)
tyre pressure	der Reifendruck
air pressure	der Luftdruck
battery	die Batterie(n)
oil	das Öl
petrol, fuel	das Benzin
diesel	das Diesel(benzin)
to accelerate	Gas geben
to fill up with petrol	(voll)tanken *(sep)*
petrol station	die Tankstelle(n)
self service	die Selbstbedienung, sb-tanken
4-star petrol	das Super(benzin)
2-star petrol	das Normal(benzin)
lead-free petrol	das bleifreie Benzin, das Bleifreie

(equivalent to)	
AA/RAC	ADAC/AvD
broken	kaputt
to check	prüfen, nachsehen *(sep)*
to repair	reparieren
repair	die Reparatur(en)
emergency call	der Notruf(e)
garage	die Werkstatt(¨en)
tool	das Werkzeug(e)
driving licence	der Führerschein(e)
green card (insurance)	die grüne Karte(n)
occupied	besetzt
free	frei
motorway	die Autobahn(en)
warning	die Warnung(en)
caution	die Vorsicht
road works	die Baustelle(n)
danger	die Gefahr(en)
dangerous	gefährlich
legal	gesetzlich
blocked	gesperrt
diversion	die Umleitung(en)
allowed	gestattet, erlaubt

not allowed	verboten
residents only	Anlieger frei
exit, turn off	die Ausfahrt(en)
entrance	die Einfahrt(en)
priority, right of way	die Vorfahrt(en)
access, driveway	die Zufahrt(en)
forwards	vorwärts
backwards	rückwärts
one-way street	die Einbahnstraße(n)
to get in lane	sich einordnen *(sep)*
to keep clear	freihalten *(sep)*
to park	parken
car park	der Parkplatz(¨e)
multi-storey car park	das Parkhaus(¨er)
lay-by, picnic area	der Rastplatz(¨e)
traffic light	die Ampel(n)

HIGHER VOCABULARY

brake	die Bremse(n)
to brake	bremsen
boot	der Kofferraum(¨e)
headlight	der Scheinwerfer(-)
bulb	die Birne(n)
steering wheel	das Steuer (Steuerräder)
windscreen wiper	der Scheibenwischer(-)
windscreen	die Windschutzscheibe(n)
engine	der Motor(en)
to turn off (the engine)	(den Motor) abstellen *(sep)*
to start (the engine)	(den Motor) starten, anlassen *(sep)*
to leave (the engine) running	(den Motor) laufen lassen
spark-plug	die Zündkerze(n)
vehicle	das Fahrzeug(e)
scooter	der Roller(-)
delivery van	der Lieferwagen(-)
breakdown vehicle	der Abschleppwagen(-)

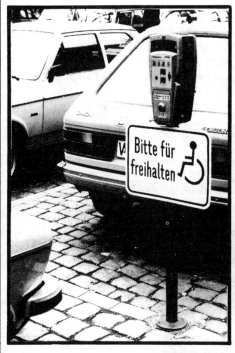

(HIGHER VOCABULARY)

to tow away	**abschleppen** *(sep)*
break-down	**die Panne(n)**
flat tyre	**die Reifenpanne(n)**
to burst	**platzen**
fault	**der Fehler(-)**
in order	**in Ordnung**
oil change	**der Ölwechsel(-)**
to estimate	**schätzen**
to hitch-hike	**trampen, per Anhalter fahren**
accident	**der Unfall("e)**
collision	**der Zusammenstoß("e)**
to run over	**überfahren**
insurance	**die Versicherung(en)**
fine	**die (Geld)strafe(n)**
fee	**die Gebühr(en)**
toll payable	**gebührenpflichtig**
to keep your distance	**Abstand halten**

speed	**die Geschwindigkeit(en)**
to drive very slowly	**Schritt fahren**
to overtake	**überholen**
traffic	**der Verkehr**
through traffic	**der Durchgangsverkehr**
traffic jam, hold-up	**der (Verkehrs)stau(s),**
motorway merging point	**das Autobahndreieck(e)**
motorway intersection	**das Autobahnkreuz(e)**
underground car park	**die Tiefgarage(n)**
no parking	**das Parkverbot(e)**
car wash	**die Autowäsche(n)**
parking meter	**die Parkuhr(en)**
to turn off	**abbiegen** *(sep)*
wet conditions	**die Nässe**
pelican crossing	**die Fußgängerampel(n)**
crossing warden	**der Schülerlotse(n)**
signposted	**ausgeschildert**

BASIC PHRASES

40 marks worth of 4-star petrol, please.	**Für 40 Mark Super, bitte.**
Please check the oil.	**Bitte prüfen Sie das Öl.**
Is there a car park near here?	**Gibt es in der Nähe einen Parkplatz?**
I've run out of petrol!	**Ich habe kein Benzin mehr!**
Can you go via Bonn?	**Kann man über Bonn fahren?**

HIGHER PHRASES

Are traffic hold-ups likely?	**Ist mit Staus zu rechnen?**
Can you put a new bulb in?	**Können Sie eine neue Birne einsetzen?**
There has been an accident.	**Da ist ein Unfall passiert!**
My windscreen is broken.	**Meine Windschutzscheibe ist kaputt.**
Have you found the fault?	**Haben Sie den Fehler gefunden?**

8 Holidays

General description

holidays	**die Ferien** (*pl*),
	der Urlaub (*no pl*)
to go on holiday	**Urlaub machen**
exchange	**der Austausch("e)**
abroad	**das Ausland** (*no pl*)
to go abroad	**ins Ausland fahren**
plan	**der Plan("e)**
to plan	**planen**
to organise	**organisieren**
brochure	**die Broschüre(n)**
town plan	**der Stadtplan("e)**
tourist information office	**das Verkehrsamt("er)**
information	**die Auskunft("e)**
to cost	**kosten**
to reserve	**reservieren**
to stay	**bleiben**
to spend (time)	**verbringen**
to spend the night	**übernachten**
hotel	**das Hotel(s)**
guesthouse	**die Pension(en)**
youth hostel	**die Jugendherberge(n)**
camp site	**der Campingplatz("e)**
to pack	**packen**
to unpack	**auspacken** (*sep*)
suitcase	**der Koffer(-)**
luggage	**das Gepäck** (*no pl*)
customs	**der Zoll("e)**
ID card	**der Personalausweis(e)**
passport	**der Paß("sse)**
	der Reisepaß("sse)
papers	**die Papiere** (*pl*)
driving licence	**der Führerschein(e)**
green card (insurance)	**die grüne Karte(n)**

journey	**die Reise(n)**
to travel	**reisen, fahren**
picnic	**das Picknick(e)**
sunglasses	**die Sonnenbrille(n)**
camera	**der Fotoapparat(e)**
bathing costume	**der Badeanzug("e)**
suntan lotion	**die Sonnencreme(s)**
north	**Nord**
south	**Süd**
east	**Ost**
west	**West**
sea	**das Meer(e), die See**
lake	**der See(n)**
beach	**der Strand("e)**
sand	**der Sand** (*no pl*)
sandcastle	**die Sandburg(en)**
Lake Constance	**der Bodensee**
(River) Danube	**die Donau**
(River) Rhine	**der Rhein**
North Sea	**die Nordsee**
Baltic Sea	**die Ostsee**
Cologne	**Köln**
Munich	**München**
Vienna	**Wien**
Hanover	**Hannover**

stay	**der Aufenthalt(e)**
accommodation	**die Unterkunft("e)**
place	**der Ort(e)**
destination	**das Ziel(e)**
travel agent's	**das Reisebüro(s)**

(HIGHER VOCABULARY)

border	**die Grenze(n)**	worth seeing	**sehenswert**
to pay duty	**verzollen**	sight	**die Sehens-**
duty free	**zollfrei**		**würdigkeit(en)**
customs (check)	**die Zollkontrolle(n)**	sightseeing visit	**die Besichtigung(en)**
to show	**zeigen**	event	**die Veranstaltung(en)**
EC	**die EG**	to intend doing	
English Channel	**der Ärmelkanal**	something	**etwas vorhaben** *(sep)*
Mediterranean	**das Mittelmeer**	to be responsible for	**haften für** *(+ acc)*

BASIC PHRASES

I have never been to Germany.	**Ich war noch nie in Deutschland.**
This year I'm going to Italy.	**Dieses Jahr fahre ich nach Italien.**
I went with my parents.	**Ich bin mit meinen Eltern gefahren.**
I'm spending my holidays at home.	**Ich verbringe meine Ferien zu Hause.**
We usually stay on a camp site.	**Gewöhnlich bleiben wir auf einem Campingplatz.**

I visited the cathedral.	**Ich habe den Dom besichtigt.**
I intend going to Germany next year.	**Ich habe vor, nächstes Jahr nach Deutschland zu fahren.**
I have nothing to declare.	**Ich habe nichts zu verzollen.**
What is there to see?	**Was für Sehenswürdigkeiten gibt es?**
I will have to find out.	**Ich muß mich erkundigen.**

Hotel accommodation

BASIC VOCABULARY

hotel	**das Hotel**(s)
guest-house	**die Pension**(en)
inn	**das Rasthaus**(¨er)
room	**das Zimmer**(-)
single room	**das Einzelzimmer**(-)
double room	**das Doppelzimmer**(-)
comfortable	**bequem**
chambermaid	**das Zimmermädchen**(-)
to book	**buchen**
to take	**nehmen**
night	**die Nacht**(¨e)
day	**der Tag**(e)
week	**die Woche**(n)
when	**wann**
free, available	**frei**
full	**voll**
alone	**allein**
together	**zusammen**
form	**das Formular**(e)
to fill in	**ausfüllen** (sep)
registration	**die Anmeldung**(en)
reception	**der Empfang**
receptionist	**die Empfangsdame**(n)
porter	**der Portier**(s)
evening meal	**das Abendessen**(-)
breakfast	**das Frühstück** (no pl)
to have breakfast	**frühstücken**
lunch	**das Mittagessen**(-)

dining room	**der Speisesaal**(säle)
bar	**die Bar**(s)
lift	**der Lift**(e), **der Fahrstuhl**(¨e), **der Aufzug**(¨e)
shower	**die Dusche**(n)
bath	**das Bad**(¨er)
car park	**der Parkplatz**(¨e)
to park	**parken**
telephone	**das Telefon**(e)
to ring up	**telefonieren mit** (+ dat), **anrufen** (+ acc) (sep)
toilet	**die Toilette**(n), **das WC**(s), coll: **das Klo**(s)
floor	**der Stock**(Stockwerke)
key	**der Schlüssel**(-)
luggage	**das Gepäck** (no pl)
suitcase	**der Koffer**(-)
travel bag	**die Reisetasche**(n)
with	**mit**
without	**ohne**
to pay	**(be)zahlen**
to cost	**kosten**
price	**der Preis**(e)
price per person	**der Preis pro Person**

(BASIC VOCABULARY)

VAT (value added tax)	**MWS**
	(die Mehrwertsteuer)
bill	**die Rechnung(en)**
cheque	**der Scheck(s)**
traveller's cheque	**der Reisescheck(s)**
service	**die Bedienung** (*no pl*)

HIGHER VOCABULARY

half board	**die Halbpension**
full board	**die Vollpension**
inclusive	**inklusive**
included	**inbegriffen**
to inform	**mitteilen** (*sep*)
to recommend	**empfehlen**
view	**die Aussicht, der Blick**
balcony	**der Balkon(e)**
quiet	**die Ruhe**
quiet	**ruhig**
tap	**der Wasserhahn(¨e)**
with running water	**mit fließendem Wasser**
hot meals	**warme Küche**
guest room	**das Fremdenzimmer(-)**
reception	**die Anmeldung(en)**
to register	**sich anmelden** (*sep*)
to sign	**unterschreiben**
signature	**die Unterschrift(en)**
ground floor	**das Erdgeschoß(sse)**
to complain	**sich beklagen**
to work (*of machinery*)	**funktionieren**
disgraceful	**unerhört**

Hotel »Zur Alpenrose«

Familie Dr. Kathrein

6433 Oetz — Hauptstraße 39, Telefon 62 08

Erholung und Gemütlichkeit finden Sie im Hotel »Alpenrose« in Oetz. Die anerkannt gute internationale Küche und ein sehenswerter Speisesaal zählen zu den Vorzügen des Hauses. Alle Zimmer mit Dusche und WC, geheiztes Freischwimmbad — Liegewiese.

„Nicht zu Hause und doch daheim"
Sommer- und Winterferien erleben in unserem gemütlichen, neuerbauten **Gasthof**
Komfortzimmer, Personenaufzug, eigenes Hausschwimmbad, Liegewiese, Fitneßraum, sonnige, ruhige, zentrale Lage!
Bes.: Herbert und Elfi Rist
Tel.: Durchwahl von der BRD 00 43/52 83/22 50

BASIC PHRASES

Have you any rooms free?	**Haben Sie noch Zimmer frei?**
How much is a room without the evening meal?	**Was kostet ein Zimmer ohne Abendessen?**
From what time do you serve breakfast?	**Ab wann servieren Sie das Frühstück?**
I'd like a room for three nights.	**Ich möchte ein Zimmer für drei Nächte.**
Can I have the bill, please?	**Kann ich bitte die Rechnung haben?**

Can you recommend another hotel?	**Können Sie ein anderes Hotel empfehlen?**
Have you anything cheaper?	**Haben Sie etwas Billigeres?**
I wanted a room with a view.	**Ich wollte ein Zimmer mit Aussicht.**
I'll take the room on the first floor.	**Ich nehme das Zimmer im ersten Stock.**
Is the meal included?	**Ist das Essen inbegriffen?**

Camping

BASIC VOCABULARY

camping	**das Camping, das Zelten**
camp site	**der Campingplatz(¨e)**
to camp	**zelten**
tent	**das Zelt(e)**
caravan	**der Wohnwagen(-)**
arrival	**die Ankunft(¨e)**
departure	**die Abreise(n)**
site, place	**der Platz(¨e)**
office	**das Büro(s)**
camping equipment	**die Campingausrüstung(en)**
battery	**die Batterie(n)**
camping stove	**der Campingkocher(-)**
tin opener	**der Dosenöffner(-)**
rucksack	**der Rucksack(¨e)**
sleeping bag	**der Schlafsack(¨e)**
fire	**das Feuer(-)**
shadow	**der Schatten(-)**
shop	**der Laden(¨), das Geschäft(e)**
kiosk	**der Kiosk(e)**
washroom	**der Waschraum(¨e)**

HIGHER VOCABULARY

camp fire	**das Lagerfeuer(-)**
air bed	**die Luftmatratze(n)**
folding chair	**der Klappstuhl(¨e)**
folding table	**der Klapptisch(e)**
collapsible	**klappbar**
portable	**tragbar**
electric current	**der Strom**
to put up	**aufbauen *(sep)*, aufschlagen *(sep)***
to pitch a tent	**ein Zelt aufschlagen *(sep)***
to take down	**abbauen *(sep)***
to borrow	**leihen**
to hire	**ausleihen *(sep)***
rubbish	**der Abfall(¨e)**
rubbish bin	**der Abfalleimer(-)**
lights out	**die Nachtruhe**
receipt	**die Quittung(en)**
charge, fee	**die Gebühr(en)**

BASIC PHRASES

Where can you buy something here?	**Wo kann man hier einkaufen?**
Have you got room for two tents?	**Haben Sie noch Platz für zwei Zelte?**
How much is it for one night?	**Was kostet eine Nacht?**
I need a tin opener.	**Ich brauche einen Dosenöffner.**
Where is the office?	**Wo ist das Büro?**

HIGHER PHRASES

Can you hire an air bed?	**Kann man eine Luftmatratze ausleihen?**
Where should we pitch our tent?	**Wo sollen wir unser Zelt aufschlagen?**
Are camp fires allowed?	**Sind Lagerfeuer erlaubt?**
I'd prefer a place in the shade.	**Ich hätte lieber einen Platz im Schatten.**
Could I have a receipt, please?	**Könnte ich bitte eine Quittung haben?**

CAMPINGPLATZ im Erholungs- und Freizeitpark "Auf der Lach" - direkt am Rhein
Geöffnet von 15.Mai bis 15.September

CAMPINGPLATZ beim Ponyhof "Landgut Ebental"
Geöffnet von April bis Oktober.

Ihren **Abfall** geben Sie bitte in die **Abfalleimer**, und **Glas** bringen Sie natürlich nicht mit!

Animation bald auch auf Campingplätzen

Deutschlands Camper bleiben künftig bei ihrer Freizeitgestaltung auf einheimischen Plätzen nicht mehr auf sich alleine gestellt. „Animation bringt Attraktion", heißt vielmehr die jüngste Erkenntnis des Verbandes der Campingplatzhalter in Deutschland (VCD), der seinen rund 1200 Mitgliedern die Beschäftigung von sogenannten Animateuren nahelegt. „Ein Fleckchen grüne Wiese reicht heutzutage nicht mehr aus", meint VCD-Präsident Gert Petzold.

Youth hostel

BASIC VOCABULARY

youth hostel	**die Jugendherberge**(n)
wardens	**die Herbergseltern** (pl)
warden	**der Herbergsvater**(¨),
	die Herbergsmutter(¨)
guest	**der Gast**(¨e)
dormitory	**der Schlafraum**(¨e)
forbidden	**verboten**
allowed	**erlaubt**
except	**außer**
price list	**die Preisliste**(n)

HIGHER VOCABULARY

member	**das Mitglied**(er)
notice board	**das schwarze Brett**
sheet	**das Bettlaken**(-)
sheets	**die Bettwäsche**
blanket	**die Decke**(n)

BASIC PHRASES

Where can you get something to eat?	**Wo kann man hier essen?**
It is just for tonight.	**Es ist nur für heute nacht.**
How much is a shower?	**Was kostet eine Dusche?**
I've got my own sleeping bag.	**Ich habe meinen eigenen Schlafsack.**
How much is it per person?	**Was macht das pro Person?**

HIGHER PHRASES

I've booked a bed.	**Ich habe ein Bett reserviert.**
At what time is the door locked?	**Um wieviel Uhr wird abgeschlossen?**
We won't be having any meals.	**Wir nehmen keine Mahlzeiten ein.**
We'd like to hire sheets.	**Wir möchten gerne Bettwäsche leihen.**

Jugendherberge Tuttlingen

Lage des Hauses: Das Haus liegt in der Stadtmitte.
Geeignet für: Wandergruppen und Schulklassen.
Freizeitangebot: Ausflüge: Bodensee 30 km, Schwarzwald 25 km, Schwäbische Alb und Donautal (Donauversickerung), Ausflugfahrten in die Schweiz und Österreich.
Bankverbindung: Kreissparkasse Tuttlingen, BLZ 643 500 70, Konto 40 606.
Nächste Jugendherbergen: Rottweil 30 km, Singen 30 km, Villingen 35 km, Burg Wildenstein 25 km.
Wichtiger Hinweis: Die Jugendherberge ist vom 1. 10. bis 1. 4. geschlossen.

Jugendherberge
Youth Hostel

Hausordnung
für Jugendherbergen

Benutzungsbedingungen
für Jugendherbergen

D
JH

Holiday home/friend's house

BASIC VOCABULARY

to exchange	**austauschen** *(sep)*
at the house of	**bei**
penfriend	**der Brieffreund(e),**
	die Brieffreundin(nen)
host	**der Gastgeber(-)**
farm	**der Bauernhof(ᵕe),**
	das Bauernhaus(ᵕer)

HIGHER VOCABULARY

holiday flat	**die Ferienwohnung(en)**
to rent, hire	**mieten**
to hang	**aufhängen** *(sep)*
bulb	**die Glühbirne(n)**

BASIC PHRASES

I'd like to have a shower.	**Ich möchte gern duschen.**
That's very kind of you.	**Das ist sehr nett von Ihnen.**
When's breakfast?	**Wann frühstückt ihr?**
I'm staying at my penfriend's house.	**Ich wohne bei meiner Brieffreundin/meinem Brieffreund.**

HIGHER PHRASES

Where can I hang my things?	**Wo kann ich meine Sachen aufhängen?**
Is it possible to rent a flat?	**Ist es möglich, eine Wohnung zu mieten?**
The bulb isn't working.	**Die Glühbirne funktioniert nicht.**

9 Food and drink

Items of food and drink

meat	das Fleisch *(no pl)*	stewed fruit	das Kompott(e)
fish	der Fisch(e)	apple	der Apfel(¨)
chicken	das (Brat)hähnchen(-)	orange	die Apfelsine(n),
chop, cutlet	das Kotelett(s)		die Orange(n)
liver	die Leber	banana	die Banane(n)
steak	das Steak(s)	pear	die Birne(n)
beef	das Rindfleisch	peach	der Pfirsich(e)
pork	das Schweinefleisch	plum	die Pflaume(n)
veal cutlet	das Schnitzel(-)	grape	die (Wein)traube(n)
goulash	der/das Gulasch	strawberry	die Erdbeere(n)
		raspberry	die Himbeere(n)
sausage	die Wurst(¨e)	cherry	die Kirsche(n)
selection of		lemon	die Zitrone(n)
sliced sausage	der Aufschnitt *(no pl)*		
sausage for frying	die Bratwurst(¨e)	vegetable	das Gemüse
curried sausage	die Currywurst(¨e)	pea	die Erbse(n)
liver sausage	die Leberwurst(¨e)	bean	die Bohne(n)
bockwurst	die Bockwurst(¨e)	onion	die Zwiebel(n)
ham	der Schinken(-)	carrot	die Karotte(n),
egg	das Ei(er)		die gelbe Rübe(n)
boiled egg	das gekochte Ei(er)	cabbage	der Kohl (Kohlköpfe)
a soft-boiled egg	ein weiches Ei(er)	pickled cabbage	das Sauerkraut *(no pl)*
a hard-boiled egg	ein hartes Ei(er)	potato	die Kartoffel(n)
fried egg	das Spiegelei(er)	fried potatoes	die Bratkartoffeln
scrambled eggs	das Rührei/die	boiled potatoes	die Salzkartoffeln
	Rühreier	potato salad	der Kartoffelsalat(e)
omelette	das Omelett(s)	chips	die Pommes Frites
milk	die Milch	crisps	die Chips
(whipped) cream	die (Schlag)sahne	rice	der Reis
ice cream	das Eis *(no pl)*	pasta	die Nudeln
yoghurt	der Joghurt(s)		
cheese	der Käse (Käsesorten)	blancmange	der Pudding(e)
soup	die Suppe(n)	vanilla	Vanille
tomato soup	die Tomatensuppe(n)	custard	der Vanillepudding(e)
		gateau	die Torte(n)
fruit	das Obst *(no pl)*	cake	der Kuchen(-)

(BASIC VOCABULARY)

biscuit	der Keks(e)
sweet	das Bonbon(s)
chewing gum	der Kaugummi(s)
chocolate	die Schokolade(n)
chocolates/praline	die Praline(n)
bread	das Brot(e)
bread roll	das Brötchen(-)
sandwich	das belegte Brot(e)
cheese sandwich	das Käsebrot(e)
ham sandwich	das Schinkenbrot(e)
black bread	das Schwarzbrot(e)
brown bread	das Graubrot(e)
white bread	das Weißbrot(e)
butter	die Butter *(no pl)*
margarine	die Margarine(n)
honey	der Honig *(no pl)*
jam	die Marmelade(n)
sugar	der Zucker *(no pl)*
oil	das Öl(e)
drink	das Getränk(e)
water	das Wasser *(no pl)*
mineral water	das Mineralwasser
juice	der Saft(¨e)
applejuice	der Apfelsaft(¨e)
cola	die Cola(s)
coke	das Coke(s)
lemonade	die Limonade(n), der Sprudel(-)
coffee	der Kaffee *(no pl)*
tea	der Tee *(no pl)*
cocoa	der Kakao(s)
alcohol	der Alkohol *(no pl)*
beer	das Bier(-)
brown ale	ein Dunkles (zwei Dunkle)
lager	ein Helles (zwei Helle)
pils	ein Pils(-)
wine	der Wein(e)
red wine	der Rotwein(e)
white wine	der Weißwein(e)

HIGHER VOCABULARY

pepper	der Pfeffer
salt	das Salz
sauce, gravy	die Soße(n)
mustard	der Senf
cauliflower	der Blumenkohl *(no pl)*
mushroom	der Champignon(s), der Pilz(e)
cucumber	die Gurke(n)
mashed potato	der Kartoffelbrei(e)
dumpling	der Knödel(-)
trout	die Forelle(n)
selection of cold meats	die kalte Platte(n)
roast	der Braten(-)
stew	der Eintopf(¨e)
lamb	das Lammfleisch
veal	das Kalbfleisch
oxtail soup	die Ochsenschwanzsuppe(n)
chicken broth	die Hühnerbrühe(n)
hamburger	der Hamburger(-)
beefsteak	das Beefsteak(s)
biscuits	das Gebäck
schnaps (strong spirit)	der Schnaps(¨e)
sparkling wine	der Sekt *(no pl)*

What items are on offer?

Restaurants and cafés

BASIC VOCABULARY

café	das Café(s), das Kaffeehaus(¨er) (*Austrian*)	to be thirsty	Durst haben, durstig sein
inn	das Gasthaus(¨er), der Gasthof(¨e)	full up	satt
restaurant	die Gaststätte(n), das Restaurant(s)	to taste	schmecken
		to smell	riechen
snack bar	die Imbißstube(n), der Schnellimbiß(sse)	to cut	schneiden
		to eat	essen
hot dog stand	der Würstchen-stand(¨e)	to chew	kauen
		to drink	trinken
bar	die Bar(s)	to swallow	schlucken
wine bar	die Weinstube(n), der Weinkeller(-)	meal	die Mahlzeit(en)
		food	das Essen(-)
service station (motorway)	der Rasthof(¨e), die Raststätte(n)	breakfast	das Frühstück(*no pl*)
		lunch	das Mittagessen(-)
waiter	der Ober(-), der Kellner(-)	to breakfast	frühstücken
		to have lunch	zu Mittag essen
waitress	die Kellnerin(nen)	dinner, evening meal	das Abendessen(-)
service	die Bedienung (*no pl*)	to have dinner	zu Abend essen
table	der Tisch(e)	supper	das Abendbrot (*no pl*)
free	frei	portion	die Portion(en)
to book	reservieren	child's portion	der Kinderteller(-)
menu	die Speisekarte(n)	to grill	grillen
set meal	das Menü(s)	to pass, to be enough	reichen
menu of the day	die Tageskarte(n)	to take away	zum Mitnehmen
wine list	die Weinkarte(n)	to pay	(be)zahlen
to order	bestellen	tip	das Trinkgeld(er)
		bill	die Rechnung(en)
cheers!	Prost!	price	der Preis(e)
enjoy the meal	Guten Appetit!	together	zusammen
delicious	lecker, köstlich		
sweet	süß	more	mehr
sour	sauer	less	weniger
hot, spicy	scharf	some	etwas, einige
		some more	noch etwas
hunger	der Hunger	a little	ein bißchen
to be hungry	Hunger haben, hungrig sein	enough	genug
		too	zu
thirst	der Durst	another	ander

(BASIC VOCABULARY)			
knife	das Messer(-)	course	der Gang("e)
fork	die Gabel(n)	wine waiter	der Weinkellner(-),
spoon	der Löffel(-)		der Getränkekellner(-)
plate	der Teller(-)	tray	das Tablett(s)
cup	die Tasse(n)	bowl	die Schüssel(n)
saucer	die Untertasse(n)	dish	die Schale(n)
glass	das Glas("er)	straw	der Strohhalm(e)
jug	das Kännchen(-)		

HIGHER VOCABULARY

		to offer	(an)bieten (*sep*)
		to recommend	empfehlen
pub (*approx. equivalent*)	die Kneipe(n),	to pour	einschenken (*sep*)
	die Schenke(n),	to try	probieren
	das Wirtshaus("er),	included	inbegriffen,
	die Wirtschaft(en)		einschließlich,
bar, counter	die Theke(n)		inklusive
table reserved for			
regulars	der Stammtisch(e)		
		baked	gebacken
starter	die Vorspeise(n)	roasted/fried	gebraten
dessert	die Nachspeise(n),	covered in breadcrumbs	paniert
	der Nachtisch(e)	mixed	gemischt

Is this a restaurant?

BASIC PHRASES

Have you a table for three?	**Haben Sie einen Tisch für drei?**
I'd like the menu, please.	**Die Speisekarte, bitte.**
Two portions of chicken, please.	**Zweimal Brathähnchen, bitte.**
Could I have some bread, please?	**Könnte ich bitte etwas Brot haben?**
Please pass the salt.	**Reichen Sie mir bitte das Salz.**
Thanks, that's enough.	**Danke, das reicht.**
The bill, please!	**Zahlen, bitte!**
Keep the change.	**Das stimmt so.**

HIGHER PHRASES

Could you tell me what 'Bockwurst' is?	**Können Sie mir bitte sagen, was „Bockwurst" ist?**
I haven't booked a table.	**Ich habe keinen Tisch reserviert.**
That tasted delicious.	**Das war prima./Das schmeckte köstlich.**
Is the service charge included?	**Ist die Bedienung inbegriffen?**
What can you recommend?	**Was empfehlen Sie?**

TEST

Sage mir wie du frühstückst...

Frage 1: Wann stehst du für gewöhnlich morgens auf?

a. Morgens? Morgens gehe ich ins Bett!	O
b. 6 Uhr	O
c. Wenn ich wach werde.	O
d. Zwischen 9 und 11 Uhr.	O

Frage 2: Warum?

a. Weil der Hahn kräht.	O
b. Weil mein Chef anruft.	O
c. Weil ich Durst habe.	O
d. Weil mein Butler klopft.	O

Frage 3: Was machst du dann?

a. Ich spurte zur Straßenbahnhaltestelle.	O
b. Ich mache erstmal 'ne Dose Bier auf.	O
c. Ich mache Frühstück.	O
d: Ich gehe immer frühstücken.	O

Frage 4: Was gibt's zu essen?

a. Nix	O
b. Hab' ich doch schon beantwortet, 'ne Dose Bier.	O
c. Meerrettich, Lachs, Champagner, Roter Kaviar...	O
d. Noch'n Toast, noch'n Ei, noch'n Kaffee, noch'n Brei..	O

Frage 5: Was liest du beim Frühstück?

a. Rheinische Post	O
b. Express	O
c. Das Etikett der Bierdose	O
d. die Prawda	O

Frage 6: Worüber redest du?

a. Politik, Religion, Wirtschaft.	O
b. Reden? Mit wem?	O
c. Das Wetter, über Leute, die gerade nicht da sind...	O
d. Theaterpremieren, Vernissagen, Mode, Philosophie...	O

Frage 7: Wieviel gibst du täglich für dein Frühstück aus?

a. 10,50 Mark	O
b. Zwischen 2 und 40 Mark	O
c. Weiß' nicht, zahle mit Diners Club.	O
d. 1,29 Mark	O

Frage 8: Was machst du nach dem Frühstück?

a. Ich gehe zur Arbeit.	O
b. Ich gehe zum Frühschoppen.	O
c. 00, mit Zeitung.	O
d. Ich gehe ins Bett.	O

Now turn to page 80 . . .

10 Shopping

General description

shop	der **Laden**(¨), das **Geschäft**(e)
to go shopping	**einkaufen** (*sep*), **Einkäufe machen**
shopkeeper	der **Händler**(-), der **Kaufmann** (**Kaufleute**)
customer	der **Kunde**(n), die **Kundin**(nen)
to buy	**kaufen**
to sell	**verkaufen**
opening hours	die **Öffnungszeiten**, die **Geschäftszeiten**
open	**geöffnet**
closed	**geschlossen**
list	die **Liste**(n)
sale	der **Schlußverkauf**(¨e)

entrance	der **Eingang**(¨e)
exit	der **Ausgang**(¨e)
price	der **Preis**(e)
special price	der **Sonderpreis**(e)
special offer	das **Sonderangebot**(e)
value for money	**preiswert**
free	**kostenlos**
to cost	**kosten**
till	die **Kasse**(n)
to pay	**(be)zahlen**
cash	das **Bargeld**
change	das **Kleingeld**
coin	die **Münze**(n)
note	der **Schein**(e)
altogether	**zusammen**
purse	das **Portemonnaie**(s), der **Geldbeutel**(-)
cheque	der **Scheck**(s)

chemist's	die **Apotheke**(n)
chemist's (non-dispensing)	die **Drogerie**(n)
hairdresser's	der **Friseursalon**(s)
department store	das **Kaufhaus**(¨er), das **Warenhaus**(¨er)
supermarket	der **Supermarkt**(¨e)
newspaper stand	der **Zeitungsstand**(¨e)
bookshop	der **Buchladen**(¨)
baker's	die **Bäckerei**(en)
butcher's	die **Fleischerei**(en), die **Metzgerei**(en)
cake shop, patisserie	die **Konditorei**(en)
grocer's	das **Lebensmittelgeschäft**(e)
market	der **Markt**(¨e)

to show	**zeigen**
to need	**brauchen**
to get	**bekommen**
to fetch	**holen**
to serve (oneself)	**(sich) bedienen**
vending machine	der **Automat**(en)
item, thing	die **Sache**(n), das **Ding**(e)

box	die **Schachtel**(n)
bottle	die **Flasche**(n)
tin	die **Dose**(n)
tin opener	der **Dosenöffner**(-)
packet	das **Paket**(e)
small packet	das **Päckchen**(-)
glass, jar	das **Glas**(¨er)
piece, item	das **Stück**

(BASIC VOCABULARY)

tube	die Tube(n)
bag	die Tüte(n)
carton, tub	der Becher(-)
kilo	das Kilo
pound	das Pfund
litre	der Liter(-)
one and a half	eineinhalb; anderthalb
	(hours and pounds only)
present, gift	das Geschenk(e)
souvenir	das Andenken(-),
	das Souvenir(s)
postcard	die Postkarte(n),
	die Ansichtskarte(n)
record	die (Schall)platte(n)
perfume	das Parfum(s)
soap	die Seife(n)
toothpaste	die Zahnpasta(pasten)
bag	die Tasche(n)
handbag	die Handtasche(n)
hairbrush	die Haarbürste(n)
(colour) film	der (Farb)film(e)
camera	der Fotoapparat(e)
jewelry	der Schmuck
	(Schmuckstücke)
chain	die Kette(n)
necklace	die (Hals)kette(n)
keyring	der Schlüsselring(e)
watch	die Armbanduhr(en)
cigarette lighter	das Feuerzeug(e)

HIGHER VOCABULARY

business holidays	die Betriebsferien (pl)
day off (hotels, pubs, etc.)	der Ruhetag(e)
shopping centre	das Einkaufszentrum (zentren)
shop window	das Schaufenster(-)
stationer's	die Schreibwaren-handlung(en)
dry cleaner's	die (Schnell)-reinigung(en)
book shop	die Buchhandlung(en)

section, department	die Abteilung(en)
ground floor	das Erdgeschoß(sse)
basement	das Untergeschoß(sse)
escalator	die Rolltreppe(n)
post office	das Postamt(¨er)
post code	die Postleitzahl(en)
stamp	die Briefmarke(n), das Postwert-zeichen(-)
envelope	der Briefumschlag(¨e)
by air mail	mit Luftpost
to spend	ausgeben (sep)
to deliver	liefern
to serve	(be)dienen
to weigh	wiegen
to exchange	umtauschen (sep)
exchange	der Umtausch(¨e)
to choose	wählen, aussuchen (sep)
choice	die (Aus)wahl (no pl)
to complain	sich beschweren
helpful	behilflich
shopping basket	der Einkaufskorb(¨e)
shopping trolley	der Einkaufswagen(-)
receipt	der Kassenzettel(-), die Quittung(en)
reduction	der Rabatt (no pl)
deposit	die Anzahlung(en)
free	umsonst
reasonable	günstig
available	erhältlich
slice	die Scheibe(n)
half	die Hälfte(n)
to peel	schälen
washing-up liquid	das Spülmittel(-)
washing powder	das Waschpulver(-)
pot	der Topf(¨e)
instructions (for use)	die Gebrauchsan-weisung(en)

BASIC PHRASES

Do you sell stamps?	**Verkaufen Sie Briefmarken?**
I'd like a kilo of potatoes, please.	**Ich möchte ein Kilo Kartoffeln, bitte.**
I'll have the small ones.	**Ich nehme die kleinen.**
I haven't got any change.	**Ich habe kein Kleingeld.**
That's not quite right.	**Da stimmt etwas nicht.**
Have you got a bigger can?	**Haben Sie eine größere Dose?**

HIGHER PHRASES

Can you change a 100 Mark note?	**Können Sie einen Hundertmarkschein wechseln?**
I'd like to exchange this book.	**Ich möchte dieses Buch umtauschen.**
Five slices of ham, please.	**Fünf Scheiben Schinken, bitte.**
There's 10 Pfennigs back on the bottle.	**Auf der Flasche sind zehn Pfennig Pfand.**

What kind of shop is this?

Clothes and items for personal use

BASIC VOCABULARY

clothes	**die Kleider** *(pl)*
clothing	**die Kleidung** *(no pl)*
ready-to-wear clothing	**die Konfektions-kleidung,**
	die Konfektion(en)
to wear	**tragen**
to have on	**anhaben** *(sep)*
fashion	**die Mode** *(no pl)*
colour	**die Farbe(n)**
size	**die Größe(n)**
anorak	**der Anorak(s)**
jacket	**die Jacke(n)**
coat	**der Mantel(¨)**
raincoat	**der Regenmantel(¨)**
hat	**der Hut(¨e)**
glove	**der Handschuh(e)**
blouse	**die Bluse(n)**
T-shirt	**das T-Shirt(s)**
shirt	**das Hemd(en)**
tie	**die Krawatte(n),**
	coll: **der Schlips(e)**
pullover	**der Pullover(-),**
	der Pulli(s)
trousers	**die Hose(n)**
jeans	**die Jeans(-)**
skirt	**der Rock(¨e)**
dress	**das Kleid(er)**
belt	**der Gürtel(-)**
tights	**die Strumpfhose(n)**
suit	**der Anzug(¨e)**
pyjamas	**der Schlafanzug(¨e)**
swimming costume	**der Badeanzug(¨e)**
swimming trunks	**die Badehose(n)**
handkerchief	**das Taschentuch(¨er)**
sandal	**die Sandale(n)**
shoe	**der Schuh(e)**
sock	**die Socke(n)**
pair	**das Paar**

HIGHER VOCABULARY

to try on	**anprobieren** *(sep)*
boot	**der Stiefel(-)**
wellington	**der Gummistiefel(-)**
scarf	**der Schal(s)**
umbrella	**der Regenschirm(e)**
cap	**die Mütze(n)**
slipper	**der Pantoffel(n),**
	der Hausschuh(e)
suit (ladies')	**das Kostüm(e)**
underwear	**die Unterwäsche** *(no pl)*
bra	**der Büstenhalter(-),**
	der BH(s)
to iron	**bügeln**
to clean	**reinigen**
to sew	**nähen**
material	**der Stoff(e)**
genuine	**echt**
leather	**das Leder** *(no pl)*
wool	**die Wolle** *(no pl)*
cotton	**die Baumwolle** *(no pl)*
silk	**die Seide** *(no pl)*
plastic	**das Plastik** *(no pl)*,
	der Kunststoff(e)

BASIC PHRASES

I'm just looking.	**Ich schaue mich nur um.**
It's too small.	**Es ist zu klein.**
I prefer the blue one.	**Der/die/das Blaue gefällt mir besser.**
Have you the same in black?	**Haben Sie dasselbe in Schwarz?**

HIGHER PHRASES

Have you got it in one size bigger?	**Haben Sie das eine Nummer größer?**
It doesn't fit.	**Es paßt nicht.**
It doesn't go with my dress.	**Es paßt nicht zu meinem Kleid.**
Could I try it on?	**Kann ich das anprobieren?**

The new fashion for women . . .

x **Frau+Familie**

Weiblich
wie noch nie

Die Karriere-Frau ist „out", Weiblichkeit und Romantik dominieren. Das ließen die Frühjahrskollektionen der französischen Modeschöpfer erkennen. Die „großen Vier" der Haute Couture, Pierre Balmain, Pierre Cardin, Jean-Louis Scherrer und Nina Ricci, überraschten das Publikum mit luxuriösen Materialien, kunstvollen Schnitten und aufwendigen Verarbeitungen. Leichte, fließende Stoffe und verschwenderische Plissees prägten fast alle Modelle der Modezaren.

11 Health and welfare

BASIC VOCABULARY

arm	der Arm(e)	fit	fit
leg	das Bein(e)	unfit	nicht fit, *coll:* schlapp
back	der Rücken(-)	to sleep	schlafen
stomach	der Magen(¨)	healthy	gesund
belly	der Bauch(¨e)	to rest	sich ausruhen *(sep)*
hand	die Hand(¨e)		
foot	der Fuß(¨e)	to fall	fallen
finger	der Finger(-)	to break	brechen
neck	der Hals(¨e)	injured	verletzt
head	der Kopf(¨e)	to help	helfen
face	das Gesicht(er)	first aid	die erste Hilfe
ear	das Ohr(en)	emergency call	der Notruf
nose	die Nase(n)	serious	ernst
mouth	der Mund(¨er)	to die	sterben
eye	das Auge(n)	dead	tot
tooth	der Zahn(¨e)	death	der Tod

doctor	der Arzt(¨e)
dentist	der Zahnarzt(ärzte)
nurse	die Krankenschwester(n)
hospital	das Krankenhaus(¨er)
clinic	die Klinik(en)
chemist's	die Apotheke(n)
tablet	die Tablette(n)
pill	die Pille(n)
medicine	die Medizin *(no pl)*

ill, sick	krank
seasick	seekrank
homesickness	das Heimweh
illness	die Krankheit(en)
stomach ache	die Bauchschmerzen *(pl)*
'flu	die Grippe
suffering from a cold	erkältet sein
temperature	das Fieber
to hurt	wehtun *(sep)*
diarrhoea	der Durchfall
tired	müde

HIGHER VOCABULARY

body	der Körper(-)
tongue	die Zunge(n)
heart	das Herz(en)
knee	das Knie(-)
thumb	der Daumen(-)
toe	die Zehe(n)
shoulder	die Schulter(n)
blood	das Blut
breast, chest	die Brust(¨e)

health cure	die Kur(en)
spa resort	der Kurort(e)
bandage	der Verband(¨e)
(sticking) plaster	das Heftpflaster(-), das Hansaplast *(no pl)*
plaster (*e.g. for broken arm*)	der Gips(e)
injection	die Spritze(n)
drops	die Tropfen *(pl)*
thermometer	das Thermometer(-)

(HIGHER VOCABULARY)

cold, catarrh	der Schnupfen
a cold	die Erkältung(en)
hayfever	der Heuschnupfen
measles	die Masern (pl)
prescription	das Rezept(e)
to examine	untersuchen
to treat	behandeln
to look after	pflegen
to pay attention to	achten auf (+ acc)
patient	der Patient(en), die Patientin(nen)
to bandage	verbinden
E111 certificate	der E111-Schein(e)
health insurance company	die Krankenkasse(n)
medicine	die Arznei(en), das Medikament(e)
appointment	der Termin(e)
surgery time	die Sprechstunde(n)
emergency service	der Notdienst(e)
blind	blind
deaf	taub
dumb	stumm
pale	blaß
breathless	atemlos
injured	verwundet
physically handicapped	körperbehindert
mentally handicapped	geistig behindert
constipated	verstopft
constipation	die Verstopfung(en)
drunk	betrunken
allergy	die Allergie(n)
to feel well	sich wohl fühlen
to feel unwell	sich nicht wohl fühlen
to cough	husten
to sneeze	niesen
to sweat	schwitzen
to cry	weinen
to sprain one's ankle	sich den Knöchel verstauchen
to vomit	sich übergeben, spucken

to bleed	bluten
to suffer	leiden
to convalesce	genesen
to recover	sich erholen
accident	der Unfall(¨e)
to have an accident	verunglücken
collision	der Zusammenstoß(¨e)
fire brigade	die Feuerwehr(en)
fireman	der Feuerwehrmann(¨er)
fire engine	der Feuerwehrwagen(-)
to put out (fire)	löschen
fire extinguisher	der Feuerlöscher(-)
to save	retten
operation	die Operation(en)
to fall	stürzen
to run over	überfahren
deadly danger	die Lebensgefahr
to die	unkommen (sep), ums Leben kommen

What kind of treatment do these people offer?

BASIC PHRASES

I'm hot/cold.	**Mir ist heiß/kalt.**
I am unwell.	**Mir ist nicht gut.**
I've a headache and my knee hurts.	**Ich habe Kopfweh und mein Knie tut weh.**
What's the matter?	**Was fehlt dir?/Was ist los mit dir?**
Where's the nearest doctor?	**Wo ist der nächste Arzt?**
Is it serious?	**Ist es ernst?**

HIGHER PHRASES

I've got a bad cold.	**Ich habe eine schlimme Erkältung.**
He's broken his leg.	**Er hat sich das Bein gebrochen.**
Have you any tablets for a stomach ache?	**Haben Sie Tabletten gegen Bauchschmerzen?**
My friend has had an accident.	**Mein Freund hat einen Unfall gehabt.**
I'd like to lie down for a bit.	**Ich möchte mich eine Weile hinlegen.**

12 Times, days, months, seasons

Days of the week

Monday	**Montag**
Tuesday	**Dienstag**
Wednesday	**Mittwoch**
Thursday	**Donnerstag**
Friday	**Freitag**
Saturday	**Sonnabend, Samstag**
Sunday	**Sonntag**
on Monday	**am Montag**
on Mondays	**montags**

The months

January	**Januar**
February	**Februar**
March	**März**
April	**April**
May	**Mai**
June	**Juni**
July	**Juli**
August	**August**
September	**September**
October	**Oktober**
November	**November**
December	**Dezember**

Seasons

season	**die Jahreszeit(en)**
spring	**der Frühling**
summer	**der Sommer**
autumn	**der Herbst**
winter	**der Winter**

The day

day	**der Tag(e)**
morning	**der Morgen(-)**
midday	**der Mittag(e)**
at midday	**mittags**
in the morning	**vormittags**
afternoon	**der Nachmittag(e)**
in the afternoon	**nachmittags**
evening	**der Abend(e)**
in the evening	**abends**
night	**die Nacht(¨e)**
during the night, at night	**nachts**
today	**heute**
yesterday	**gestern**
the day before yesterday	**vorgestern**
tomorrow	**morgen**
the day after tomorrow	**übermorgen**

Holidays

(bank) holiday	**der Feiertag(e)**
Christmas	**Weihnachten**
Christmas Eve	**der heilige Abend**
New Year's Eve	**Silvester**
New Year	**Neujahr**
Easter	**Ostern**
Whitsun	**Pfingsten**
carnival	**der Karneval, der Fasching, die Fastnacht**

Time/periods of time

time	**die Zeit(en),**		week	**die Woche(n)**
	die Uhrzeit(en)		fortnight	**vierzehn Tage,**
hour	**die Stunde(n)**			**zwei Wochen**
minute	**die Minute(n)**		month	**der Monat(e)**
second	**die Sekunde(n)**		year	**das Jahr(e)**
half	**halb**		century	**das Jahrhundert(e)**
quarter	**das Viertel(-)**		previous	**vorig**

PHRASES

What time is it?	**Wieviel Uhr ist es?/Wie spät ist es?**
It is half past three.	**Es ist halb vier.**
It is a quarter to four.	**Es ist Viertel vor vier./Es ist dreiviertel vier.**
What date is it?	**Welches Datum haben wir heute?**
Today is May 4th.	**Heute ist der vierte Mai.**
In the summer	**Im Sommer**
Every Sunday	**Jeden Sonntag**
Tomorrow and the day after	**Morgen und übermorgen**
He will arrive on April 3rd.	**Er kommt am dritten April an.**
Spring begins in a fortnight.	**In zwei Wochen ist Frühlingsanfang.**

Badezeit: 2 Stunden
Öffnungszeiten des Hallenbades:
Montags, Dienstag, Mittwochs und Freitags: von 8,00 bis 21,00 Uhr
Donnerstags: von 8,00 bis 18,00 Uhr
Samstags: von 9,00 bis 19,00 Uhr
Sonntags: von 8,00 bis 13,00 Uhr

Wir beraten Sie auch vom
27.12. – 30.12.88
täglich von 9 – 12 und 14 – 16 Uhr

Auf dem gesamten
Münsterplatz

werktags 5 – 19 Uhr

frei mit Parkscheibe
bis 2 Stunden
werktags von 9 bis 19 Uhr

13 Geography and the weather

Buildings/places around town

station	**der Bahnhof(¨e)**
bus station	**der Busbahnhof(¨e)**
port, harbour	**der Hafen(¨)**
airport	**der Flughafen(¨)**
hotel	**das Hotel(s)**
travel agent's	**das Reisebüro(s)**
tourist information office	**das Verkehrsamt(¨er)**
castle	**das Schloß(¨sser)**
medieval castle	**die Burg(en)**
tower	**der Turm(¨e)**
church	**die Kirche(n)**
cathedral	**der Dom(e)**
museum	**das Museum(Museen)**
theatre	**das Theater(-)**
cinema	**das Kino(s)**
library	**die Bibliothek(en)**
swimming pool	**das Schwimmbad(¨er)**
indoor swimming pool	**das Hallenbad(¨er)**
outdoor swimming pool	**das Freibad(¨er)**
stadium	**das Stadion(Stadien)**
town hall	**das Rathaus(¨er)**
clinic	**die Klinik(en)**
hospital	**das Krankenhaus(¨er)**
police station	**die Polizeiwache(n)**
post office	**die Post (Postämter)**
the old town	**die Altstadt(¨e)**
the new town	**die Neustadt(¨e)**
capital city	**die Hauptstadt(¨e)**
town centre	**die Stadtmitte(n),**
	das Stadtzentrum
	(zentren)

square	**der Platz(¨e)**
market square	**der Marktplatz(¨e)**
town wall	**die Stadtmauer(n)**
road	**die Straße(n)**
'B' road	**die Landstraße(n)**
'A' road	**die Bundesstraße(n)**
motorway	**die Autobahn(en)**
crossroads	**die Kreuzung(en)**
bridge	**die Brücke(n)**
car park	**der Parkplatz(¨e)**
multi-storey car park	**das Parkhaus(¨er)**
petrol station	**die Tankstelle(n)**
traffic lights	**die Ampel(n)**
building site	**die Baustelle(n)**
bus stop	**die Bushaltestelle(n)**
phone booth	**die Telefonzelle(n)**
pavement	**der Bürgersteig(e)**
pedestrian precinct	**die Fußgängerzone(n)**

letter box	**der Briefkasten(¨)**
zebra crossing	**der Zebrastreifen(-)**
level crossing	**der Bahnübergang(¨e)**
signpost	**der Wegweiser(-)**
escalator	**die Rolltreppe(n)**
inhabitant	**der Einwohner(-)**
district	**der Kreis(e),**
	der Bezirk(e)
area	**das Gebiet(e),**
	die Gegend(en)
place	**der Ort(e)**
part of town	**der Stadtteil(e)**

(HIGHER VOCABULARY)

twin town	die Partnerstadt(¨e)	ruin	die Ruine(n)
suburb	der Vorort(e)	cemetery	der Friedhof(¨e)
high-rise block	das Hochhaus(¨er)	grave	das Grab(¨er)
monument	das Denkmal(¨er)		

BASIC PHRASES

How do I get to the library?	Wie komme ich zur Bibliothek?
It is opposite the cathedral.	Sie ist gegenüber dem Dom.
Is there an old town?	Gibt es eine Altstadt?
Have you got a map of the area?	Haben Sie eine Karte von der Gegend?
Where is the nearest car park?	Wo ist der nächste Parkplatz?

HIGHER PHRASES

Turn left at the town hall.	Biegen Sie am Rathaus links ab.
How many inhabitants has the town?	Wie viele Einwohner hat die Stadt?
My hometown is in an industrial area.	Meine Heimatstadt liegt in einem Industriegebiet.
I live in a suburb of Manchester.	Ich wohne in einem Vorort von Manchester.
You go past a monument.	Sie gehen an einem Denkmal vorbei.

Which building is open 24 hours?

Fernsehturm, Telefon 43 80 24 [C 4]
Gesamthöhe 271,5 m, Aussichtsplattform in 128 m Höhe
rotierendes Restaurant in 132 m Höhe
Aussichtsplattform täglich geöffnet von 10.00 bis 23.00 Uhr
Eintritt: Erwachsene 3,75 DM, Kinder bis zu 12 Jahren 2,50 DM
Restaurant täglich geöffnet von 12.00 bis 23.00 Uhr

Rathaus, Telefon 3 68 11 [E 5]
Führungen montags bis freitags 10.00 bis 15.00 Uhr,
sonnabends und sonntags 10.00 bis 13.00 Uhr halbstündlich,
fremdsprachliche Führungen (englisch und französisch) montags bis freitags
10.15 bis 15.15 Uhr, sonnabends und sonntags 10.15 bis 13.15 Uhr stündlich.
Keine Führungen bei offiziellen Veranstaltungen (es empfiehlt sich telefoni-
sche Rückfrage) und an den 1. Feiertagen zu Ostern, Pfingsten u. Weihnachten.
Preis 1 DM.

POSTAMT **Im Hauptbahnhof:** Tag und Nacht geöffnet
Im Flughafen: 7 bis 21 Uhr, So. 9 bis 20 Uhr
Im Bahnhof Harburg: 6 bis 22 Uhr, Sa/So 6 bis 21 Uhr
Postwertzeichen, Telegramme, Ferngespräche, Einschreiben,
Postsparkasse.
Kaltenkirchener Straße 1, Hamburg-Altona:
8-19, Sa. 8-12, So 11-12 Uhr — Annahme von Paketen und Päckchen

Nature and location

BASIC VOCABULARY

country	das Land(¨er)
countryside	die Landschaft(en)
hill	der Hügel(-)
mountain	der Berg(e)
high	hoch
valley	das Tal(¨er)
stone	der Stein(e)
hole	das Loch(¨er)
nature	die Natur
field	das Feld(er)
meadow	die Wiese(n)
woods, forest	der Wald(¨er)
park	der Park(s)
quiet	ruhig, still
tree	der Baum(¨e)
flower	die Blume(n)
sea	das Meer(e), die See
lake	der See(n)
river	der Fluß(¨sse)
to flow	fließen
deep	tief
island	die Insel(n)
beach	der Strand(¨e)
sand	der Sand (no pl)
clean	sauber
dirty	schmutzig

HIGHER VOCABULARY

area	die Umgebung(en), die Gegend(en)
coast	die Küste(n)
stream	der Bach(¨e)
dam	die Talsperre(n)
bank	das Ufer(-)
mountain range	das Gebirge(-)
steep	steil
summit	der Gipfel(-)
flat	flach
park	die (Park)anlage(n)
plant	die Pflanze(n)
fly	die Mücke(n), die Fliege(n)

Erst wenn der letzte Baum gerodet der letzte Fluß vergiftet der letzte Fisch gefangen werdet ihr feststellen daß man Geld nicht essen kann

In tiefer Trauer geben wir bekannt, daß auch dieser lebensnotwendige Nadelbaum

Fichte
(Luftfilter)

seiner Aufgabe nicht mehr gewachsen ist. Schwefeldioxid, Saurer Regen und Ozon sind ihm zum Verhängnis geworden. Die Verabschiedung findet täglich statt. Bitte keine Kranzspenden, sondern eine saubere Umwelt für seine Kinder.

BASIC PHRASES

I live in the country.	Ich wohne auf dem Land.
The country is so clean.	Das Land ist so sauber.
I live by the sea.	Ich wohne am Meer.

HIGHER PHRASES

There are a lot of flies in this area.	In dieser Gegend gibt es viele Mücken.
The castle has a beautiful park.	Zum Schloß gehört eine schöne Parkanlage.

Weather

BASIC VOCABULARY

weather	das Wetter
sky	der Himmel
degree	der Grad(e)
centigrade	Grad Celsius
shade	der Schatten(-)
wind	der Wind(e)
windy	windig
thunderstorm	das Gewitter(-)
storm	der Sturm(¨e)
stormy	stürmisch
cloud	die Wolke(n)
cloudy	wolkig
thunder	der Donner
to thunder	donnern
lightning	der Blitz(e)
to flash with lightning	blitzen
rain	der Regen
to rain	regnen
rainy	regnerisch
wet	naß
cool	kühl
to freeze	(ge)frieren
snow	der Schnee
to snow	schneien
ice	das Eis
sun	die Sonne
sunny	sonnig
to shine	scheinen
sunshine	der Sonnenschein
warm	warm
hot	heiß
lovely, wonderful	herrlich

HIGHER VOCABULARY

fog	der Nebel
foggy	neblig
mild	mild

bright	heiter
sultry	schwül
dry	trocken
changeable	veränderlich
shower	der Schauer(-)
rain	der Niederschlag(¨e)
damp, wet	feucht
overcast	trüb
cloudy	bewölkt
to hail	hageln
hail	der Hagel
awful weather	das schlechte Wetter, coll: das Sauwetter
cold	die Kälte
heat	die Hitze
climate	das Klima(s)
front	die Front(en)
star	der Stern(e)
moon	der Mond(e)
weather forecast	die Wetterlage(n), die Wettervorhersage(n), der Wetterbericht(e)
brightening up	die Aufheiterung(en)
cloud	die Bewölkung
cloudless	wolkenlos
high pressure	der Hochdruck
low pressure	der Tiefdruck
(day's) highest temperature	die (Tages)höchsttemperatur(en)
(day's) lowest temperature	die (Tages)tiefsttemperatur(en)
remaining cool	weiterhin kühl

BASIC PHRASES

Lovely weather today!	**Herrliches Wetter heute!**
That was a bad storm.	**Das war ein schlimmer Sturm.**
It's raining heavily.	**Es regnet stark.**
The sun is shining.	**Die Sonne scheint.**
It was 35° in the shade.	**Es war 35 Grad im Schatten.**

HIGHER PHRASES

What's the weather forecast like?	**Wie ist die Wettervorhersage?**
I hope it will stay dry.	**Hoffentlich bleibt es trocken.**
It looks rainy.	**Es sieht nach Regen aus.**
On a foggy autumn day	**An einem nebligen Herbsttag**

What's the weather like today?

Deutscher Wetterdienst

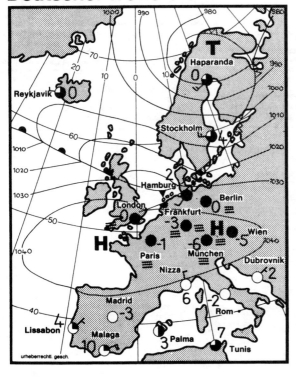

Zeichenerklärung:	
○	wolkenlos
◗	heiter
◑	halb bedeckt
◕	wolkig
●	bedeckt
⚲	Nordwind 10 km/h
⚲⌐	Ostwind 20 km/h
⚲	Südwind 30 km/h
⚲●	Westwind 40 km/h
Temperatur in Grad Celsius	
≡	Nebel
❥	Sprühregen
●	Regen
⌒⌣	gefrierender Regen
✳	Schnee
▼	Schauer
⎡Ƶ	Gewitter
///.	Niederschlagsgebiet
▲▲	Warmfront
⌒⌒	Okklusion
▲▲	Kaltfront am Boden
△△	Kaltfront in der Höhe
⇨	Luftströmung warm
⬛⇨	Luftströmung kalt
H	Hochdruckzentrum
T	Tiefdruckzentrum
h	Sekundär Hoch
t	Sekundär Tief
⌒⌒	Isobaren

You may need help from your teacher . . .

TEST

Auswertung:
Frage: 1 2 3 4 5 6 7 8

	1	2	3	4	5	6	7	8
a	5	5	3	3	3	3	3	3
b	1	3	1	1	5	1	5	7
c	7	1	5	7	1	5	7	5
d	3	7	7	5	7	7	1	1

0 - 12 Punkte
Penner. Du lebst nicht, du vegetierst. Trink' erstmal dein Bier aus und nach den Test nochmal. Wenn du dann immer noch so ein blödes Ergebnis hast, dann gib dich in Behandlung, sonst ist dein Leben nicht mehr die Butter aufs Brot wert. Du hast ein Problem, könnte man sagen, trifft aber wohl nicht ganz zu, du hast eher einen ganzen Korb voller Probleme. Bemühe dich. Erst wenn du es schaffst, dir am morgen ein Marmeladenbrötchen mit ruhiger Hand zu bereiten und es dann auch aufzuessen, bist du aus dem Gröbsten raus.

13 - 25 Punkte
Nun ja. Du bemühst dich. Du lebst halt wie du es gelernt hast und kommst auch ganz gut damit klar. Aber du bist gehemmt, du gehst nicht aus dir heraus. Arbeite an deinem Selbstbewußtsein. Du mußt es schaffen, den Mut aufzubringen, den Kellner nach einer neuen Gabel zu schicken, wenn deine dir hingefallen ist, anstatt sie verstohlen an der Serviette abzuwischen. Du mußt dich auch mal trauen, deinem Chef eine ganz schrille Ausrede aufzutischen, wenn du zwei Stunden zu spät kommst. Erst wenn du deine vierte Großmutter beer-

digt hast, wird er deine unerschrockene Art zu schätzen und zu entlohnen wissen. Du schaffst das.
Tip: Jeden zweiten Tag ein weichgekochtes Ei, weniger Kaffee, lieber mal ein Glas Sekt.

25 - 43 Punkte
Du bist in Ordnung. Wer so frühstückt wie du, hat auch sonst die Zeichen der Zeit verstanden.
Easy going: was du zwischen 10 und 11 Uhr nicht schaffst, kannst du immer noch zwischen 16 und 17 Uhr auf den nächsten Tag verschieben. Du mußt nur ein wenig aufpassen, daß du mit deiner ständig guten Laune deinen Mitmenschen nicht zu sehr auf den Keks gehst. Ansonsten weiter so.
Zur Belohnung für dein gutes Ergebnis darfst du aus unserer Frühstücksliste ein nettes Lokal aussuchen und die Redaktion bei Gelegenheit einladen. Danke auch.

44 - 56 Punkte
Angeber. Strunzkopp. Instant-Ultra. Wir glauben dir sowieso nur die Hälfte deiner Antworten und wenn die stimmen, dann möge Lukullus dafür sorgen, daß dir Kaviar und Lachs aus den Ohren wieder rauskommen, Schnösel. Kultur und Kohle wiedersprechen sich bisweilen. Wer so wie du den Tag beginnt, der kann sie ja auch sonst nicht alle an der Waffel haben, ehrlich. Dich sollte man mit schwarzem, ungezuckerten Kaffee kurieren. In aller Öffentlichkeit natürlich, damit dein künstliches Image gleich mittherapiert wird. Aber wir wollen mal nicht so sein: Vier Wochen Bircher-Müsli und dann langsam wieder mit Schinken und Salami anfangen. Ist das klar?!